What Now?

Words of Wisdom for Life After Graduation

Jennifer Leigh Selig

MJF BOOKS
NEW YORK

Published by MJF Books
Fine Communications
322 Eighth Avenue
New York, NY 10001

What Now?
LC Control Number 2002116474
ISBN 1-56731-610-7

This edition published in arrangement with Andrews McMeel Publishing,
an Andrews McMeel Universal company.

Manufactured in the United States of America on acid-free paper ∞

MJF Books and the MJF colophon are trademarks of Fine Creative
Media, Inc.

VB   10   9   8   7   6   5   4   3   2   1

DEDICATION

To my family:

My true teachers, and the apples of my eye. To Hayley and Hayden, this teacher's pets.

To the students of Dixon High School, past and present:

You have made me laugh, driven me nuts, touched my soul, taught me the meaning of love, and made me strive to be a better teacher and human being for you. Each one of your names is carved indelibly upon my heart, and this book is especially for you.

And to my God:

For calling.

Contents

Introduction

As a high school teacher for the last ten years, I have watched thousands of students go through one of the last remaining rites of passage our culture maintains for youth—the rite we call graduation. I have seen them enter as freshmen, when graduation seems a lifetime away; I have seen them become sophomores and taste the bit of freedom that comes with being "upper" lower classmen; I have seen them as juniors relishing the inevitable feeling that they will soon rule the school; and I have seen them as seniors, at the same time both scared and anxious to let go of the past, both nervous and excited about the future, both living completely in the precious present yet aware of how quickly time has slipped through their hands. In public, they are all bravado about graduation, but in private, they have often returned full circle to the panic of kindergartners who cling to their parents and plead, "Please don't make me go yet."

Yet go they must, in a ceremony full of pomp and circumstance, with those funny hats and odd gowns on the outside, and hearts fluttering with nervous anticipation and excitement on the inside.

As an adult watching this rite of passage, as an adult who can remember having been there myself, with all the attendant confusion and mixed emotions, I often wish there was something we could give to our graduates beyond just a diploma. A diploma, after all, speaks only to the past: "This is what your life has been about—this is what you have achieved. Done. Finished." But it is not by accident that the word *commencement* is synonymous with *graduation: Commencement* means a new start or beginning, implying the future rather than the past. So it seems to me that the adult community is partially derelict in our duty to our youth in handing them only words about what they did in the past at this ceremony—to truly mark commencement, we should also hand them words about what they can do in the future.

And what might those words say? Perhaps they would talk a little about letting go of the past, how to treasure it and still move on. They might acknowledge the people who made the past possible, including teachers, friends, and family. Perhaps they would muse on the meaning of success, broadening the definition beyond the achievement of a diploma to include the meaning of a successful life. They might attempt to explain what life means, then offer some advice about how to live it to the fullest. Those words might lead into the importance of dreaming to one's future, and following those dreams naturally flows into a discussion of reaching for the stars, because since antiquity people have not only wished upon the stars but also used them as symbols for our highest aspirations. And no words we give our graduates would be complete without discussing their life's work—how to listen to the call inherent in the concept of vocation, how to combine what they do for a living with what they love about living.

Toni Morrison once wrote, "If there is a book you really want to read but it hasn't been written yet, then you must write it." Here is that book—the words I wished I had been handed when I graduated, the words I wish I could hand to my students when they graduate, the words I wish we could hand to all our youth when they graduate.

Whoever handed you this book now wishes the same for you. Know that all of us in the adult community take pride in what you have achieved in the past, celebrate with you the joy and freedom of your present, and offer you the best that words from the heart can give to guide you in the future, as you ponder the question *What Now?*

Letting Go of the Past

◆ ◆ ◆

Look at what you love on graduation day. Take the classes, the friends, and the family that have inspired the most in you. Save them in your permanent memory and make a backup disk. When you remember what you love, you will remember who you are. If you remember who you are, you can do anything.

◆ *Cathy Guisewite*

When one door of happiness closes, another opens; but often we look so long at the closed door that we do not see the one which has been opened for us.

◆ *Helen Keller*

What's past is prologue.

◆ *William Shakespeare*

The world is round and the place which may seem like the end may also be only the beginning.

◆ *Ivy Baker*

Look not mournfully into the Past. It comes not back again. Wisely improve on the Present. It is thine. Go forth to meet the shadowy Future, without fear, and with a manly heart.

◆ *Henry Wadsworth Longfellow*

START HERE . . .

Your life line is a crease in the palm of your hand that is shaped from where your thumb folds in when you make a fist. My life line is broken in the middle of my left hand. When I first noticed this it scared me to tears. The friend that had told me about life lines said it was a sign that I would die. I told my mother, and she didn't make me feel any better. For some strange reason she was as concerned about what it meant as I was, and she didn't hide that concern well. That's when I decided I had AIDS.

I hadn't heard much about the deadly disease; that is, I didn't know how you got it, but I knew it was really bad. The same friend that told me about life lines had told me about AIDS. She said you got it if you were gay, or kissed someone who was the same sex as you. I had kissed my friend Melissa Novak, so that's how I got AIDS. Suddenly I took on all the symptoms. I was really weak all the time and I couldn't eat much. I started to stay home from school, sick, because I believed I was. Mom would take me to the doctor, and I went very willingly. It would be easier if he told her that I was dying than if I had to do it. When I was told over and over that nothing was wrong with me, I thought it was just because the doctor didn't know what to look for. I was too afraid to tell him I had AIDS, though, because then I would have to tell him I kissed a girl, and he would think I was disgusting. So, I went on living for the dead.

Every night before I went to sleep I would say the same prayer, that went, "Now I lay me down to sleep, I pray the Lord my soul to keep. If I should die before I wake, I pray the Lord my soul to take," just in case. I never thought I would live to graduate from high school. All because someone told me a crease in my hand was wrong.

Many years later, long after I had found out how you really got AIDS, the fear came back. This time I got a real AIDS test. This time I had a reason to be scared. But I'm still here, I'm still healthy, and this year I'm graduating from high school. Go figure.

Who Said It Was Time?

I didn't get AIDS. I'm not pregnant. I never got into a tragic accident that left me paralyzed in the hospital. I stayed in school. I never became addicted to drugs. I pursued drama. I received awards for my art. I made friends with my teachers. I never got in a fight. I lived through bad relationships, and what some people like to call the hardest part of your life. Now something I thought would never come to an end has, and I'm scared.

All the things they told me to watch out for I did. I followed the less feared path and only branched off when I felt daring. They told me to be careful when it came to drugs and sex, and I was. They said it was going to be hard, but I made it. They told me to be good, and I tried. The end is here now. I made it through in one piece. All I was scared of never happened. So why don't I feel proud?

Why am I not glad to be gone? What makes me feel lonely and worthless? Is there something more I should have done? Did they leave out a painful truth? Did I forget to read the last rule? Did someone say something I didn't hear? If everything went as well as it could have, why don't I feel like I want to leave? I didn't like it here much anyway. So, why am I crying now that I'm forced to go?

Take me back, just for a while. Just one more week. A day. I'll look at everything differently this time. Don't make me go. Don't let me cry. I'm not really supposed to leave now; it's all a big mistake. A dream. When I wake up I'll be six years old and just starting out. I'm not really leaving. I just lied to see how you'd respond. Right? It's a dream, a story.

No, it's not a dream. I am leaving. Four years of my life are over. It's time for me to go. You look at me as though I was crazy for ever being sad at leaving this place. You say you won't miss a thing. Look me in the eyes now and I'll tell you a truth . . .

You will.

◆ *Megan Biolchini*

You are told a lot about your education, but some beautiful, sacred memory, preserved since childhood, is perhaps the best education of all. If a man carries many such memories into life with him, he is saved for the rest of his days. And even if only one good memory is left in our hearts, it may also be the instrument of our salvation one day.

◆ *Fyodor Dostoyevsky*

Remembrance is the sweetest flower,
of all this world's perfuming;
memory guards it sun or shower,
friendship keeps it blooming.

◆ *Anonymous*

REGRET

In these transparent-clouded, gentle skies,
Where through the moist beams of the soft June sun
Might any moment break, no sorrow lies,
No note of grief in swollen brooks that run,
No hint of woe in this subdued, calm tone
Of all the prospect unto dreamy eyes.

Only a tender, unnamed half-regret
For the lost beauty of the gracious morn;
A yearning aspiration, fainter yet,
For brighter suns in joyous days unborn,
Now while brief showers ruffle grass and corn,
And all the earth lies shadowed, grave, and wet;

Space for the happy soul to pause again
From pure content of all unbroken bliss,
To dream the future void of grief and pain,
And muse upon the past, in reveries
More sweet for knowledge that the present is
Not all complete, with mist and clouds and rain.

◆ *Emma Lazarus*

Light tomorrow with today.

◆ *Elizabeth Barrett Browning*

You will find as you look back upon your life that the moments when you have really lived are the moments when you have done things in a spirit of love.

◆ *Henry Drummond*

The book is closed, the year is done,
The pages full of tasks begun.
A little joy, a little care,
Along with dreams, are written there.
This new day brings another year,
Renewing hope, dispelling fear.
And we may find before the end,
A deep content, another friend.

◆ *Arch Ward*

Regret for the things we did can be tempered by time; it is regret for the things we did not do that is inconsolable.

Sydney J. Harris

And ever has it been that love knows not its own depth until the hour of separation.

Kahlil Gibran

We crucify ourselves between two thieves: regret for yesterday and fear of tomorrow.

Fulton Oursler

Happy memories, like a lighted candle, light the dark places of later life.

Ruth Smeltzer

We should have no regrets.... The past is finished. There is nothing to be gained by going over it. Whatever it gave us in the experiences it brought us was something we had to know.

Rebecca Beard

I never went to high school reunions. My thing is, out of sight, out of mind. That's my attitude toward life. So I don't have any romanticism about any part of my past. I think of it only inasmuch as it gave me pleasure or helped me grow psychologically. That is the only thing that interests me about yesterday. I don't believe in yesterday, by the way. You know, I don't believe in yesterday. I am only interested in what I am doing now.

◆ *John Lennon*

Yesterday is but today's memory and tomorrow is today's dream.

◆ *Kahlil Gibran*

Of all our possessions there is only one which cannot be taken away from us, and that is memory; to let a beautiful moment slip into memory is only to keep it, not to lose it. Let the moment pass ... let go ... let go; it is yours for always.

◆ *Theodore Sturgeon*

The first recipe for happiness is: Avoid too lengthy meditations on the past.

◆ *André Maurois*

There's a trick to the Graceful Exit. It begins with the vision to recognize when a job, a life stage, a relationship is over—and to let go. It means leaving what's over without denying its validity or its past importance in our lives.

It involves a sense of future, a belief that every exit line is an entry, that we are moving on, rather than out. The trick of retiring well may be the trick of living well. It's hard to recognize that life isn't a holding action but a process. It's hard to learn that we don't leave the best parts of ourselves behind, back in the dugout or in the office. We own what we learned back there. The experiences and the growth are grafted onto our lives. And when we exit, we can take ourselves along—quite gracefully.

         Ellen Goodman

Don't be dismayed at good-byes.
A farewell is necessary
before you can meet again.
And meeting again,
after moments or lifetimes,
is certain for those
who are friends.

         Richard Bach

THE OLD DAYS WE REMEMBER

The old days we remember,
     How softly did they glide
     While all untouch'd by worldly care
     We wander'd side by side.
In those pleasant days, when the sun's last rays
     Just linger'd on the hill,
Or the moon's pale light with the coming night

Shone o'er our pathway still.
The old days we remember,—
Oh! could we but go back
To their quiet hours, and tread once more
Their bright familiar track,
Could we picture again, what we pictured then,
Of the sunny world that lay
From the green hillside, and the waters wide,
And our glad hearts far away.
A bitter sigh for the hours gone by,
The dreams that might not last,
The friends deem'd true when our hopes were new,
And the glorious visions past!

◆ *Lucy Hopper*

God gave us memory that we might have roses in December.

◆ *Sir James M. Barrie*

The past is the only dead thing that smells sweet.

◆ *Edward Thomas*

The good old days were never that good, believe me. The good new days are today, and better days are coming tomorrow. Our greatest songs are still unsung.

◆ *Hubert H. Humphrey*

Paraphrasing the words of John Kenneth Galbraith, the American economist, from a commencement address at American University, "Commencement oratory . . . must avoid anything that hints of partisan politics, political preference, sex, religion, or unduly firm opinion."

As this forced me to eliminate volumes one and two of my speech and to drastically abridge volume three, my comments will be somewhat abbreviated. But brevity is not a problem. Draft fifteen is 38 paragraphs consisting of 1,845 words. It averages 3.3 sentences per paragraph and 13.4 words per sentence. Statistically, it sounds good.

I know you have worked for thirteen years . . . dutifully filling out dittos and Scantrons, taking notes in class and reading textbooks, all in anticipation of this commencement speech.

As this speech would be thoroughly criticized by the English department were it to omit metaphor, I hereby offer one. Our development as human beings and as students has paralleled the changes in our writing instruments.

The first few years we used crayon. In those days, we had forty-eight colors to choose from. Red, orange, orchid, aquamarine, carnation pink, and brown were all options. We had so many choices: our lives had just begun. We were learning how to ride bikes, color outside of the lines, play in the sandbox, eat off the floor. Crayon was the craze.

As we matured, inch-thick pencils were "happening." Life became less carefree. We could not just color anywhere, anytime, and be left alone. Demands were made: reading became fundamental. And our teachers restricted our armory to number-ten lead pencils.

When we could handle sharp objects, the number-two pencil was introduced. A novel idea, it came with this lovely pink eraser. At this age, we were self-aware enough to recognize our mistakes. To feel, sometimes, motivated enough to correct our errors. To erase the faux pas that time would uncover.

Maturity indoctrinated us in the use of the three-color pen and Bic medium ballpoint. These implements symbolized the responsibility of our new societal roles. We were expected to make fewer errors, to be neat, to take care in our work.

Subsequently, our age brought so much latitude from the instructor that we were afforded the option of writing implements. "Pen or pencil, your choice" became the phrase in many classes.

But enough about writing instruments. I think the ink has run out on that extended metaphor.

As we sit here today, our caps and gowns envelop a medley of emotions. The word *commencement* makes these proceedings sound clear-cut. They are. A beginning.

The graduation process is not very difficult to understand. Walk in. Sit down. Listen to some speeches. Collect your diploma. Walk out. Celebrate.

We are not only ending our high school career. Most of us will soon embark upon higher education. We sit on the brink of radical change, most of us entering an atmosphere so different that it's referred to as the university rather than "higher school."

Some feel that their secondary education has not impacted them that much. "What does high school matter?"

But think about to what extent the tone of your life has been set.

Your character is defined. To some degree, your environment has helped to shape who you have become. Your parents; your mathematics teacher who you swear has a diet consisting of four different food groups: arithmetic, algebra, geometry, and calculus; your rich aunt who sends you a box of chocolates each year from the West Coast; your best friends, who you're sure are teetering between perfection and mediocrity; the psychotic pharmacist at your corner drugstore; and even your eccentric neighbor with the limp. Each of these individuals is a part of your existence.

I hope you have asked yourself, "Who am I?" I know I have asked that question of myself. I have even occasionally asked, "Who is this person?" or "Who are you?" For if you do not know who you are, that is, what your system of beliefs and morality is, who could?

A life without values is a life without definition. And life without definition is analogous to sports without rules. You cannot be sure whether anyone is winning or losing, and you cannot tell who is cheating.

The quiz for morality seems easily comprehensible. That's because it is. Ask yourself, "Self, am I a car without a steering wheel? Am I an actor without a script? Am I algebra without a variable? Am I an essay without a thesis?"

The answer of course is personal. Individual. Exclusive to you.

Who are you? You are you. As long as you know the identity of that "you," then everyone can aspire to know you and feel comfortable with who you are.

After reflection on "the true you," it becomes time to reflect upon what we have accomplished. It's time for our commencement affirmation. Since Stuart Smalley from *Saturday Night Live* was unable to attend tonight, we must forge on in his absence. Will the graduating class please repeat after me?

"I'm good enough. I'm smart enough. And doggone it, people like me."

Every graduate's deepest fear.

John Updike once said, "The Founding Fathers in their wisdom decided that children were an unnatural strain on parents. So they provided jails called schools, equipped with tortures called an education. School is where you go between when your parents can't take you and industry can't take you."

Each of you listening will respond differently to this comment. Some of my fellow inmates—excuse me, classmates—might sing out in agreement; others might remain quiet, hoping for time off for good behavior. The jailers, a.k.a. faculty, might abhor it. The wardens—I mean, the administration—might deny it. Our parents and grandparents might ramble on about the importance of a good education.

But in spite of the locked bathrooms and the roped off parking lot, the piece of paper which we patiently await (and the years of work that preceded it), will soon free us from restraints in the future. We have proven ourselves in many ways.

I interrupt this address for a public service announcement. Have you been maimed or killed in a cap-and-gown accident? Have you lost an eye in a tassel-related injury? You may deserve monetary damages. Under state law, it is illegal to throw your caps up during a commencement ceremony. See your counselor for more information about the money that you may be due.

During our quest for knowledge, we have noted that the school system does not consist of unconditional "excellence in education."

In any school, the faculty is not completely composed of effective educators. Some mathematics teachers are simply unable to function. Globally, some science teachers just do not react well with students.

Some social studies teachers have a poor pedagogical history. Some physical education teachers simply are not fit to teach. Some English teachers do not know how to read the signals of their classes. Some music teachers just do not measure up. Some foreign language instructors have too alien an approach. Some art teachers just have not learned how to sculpt a class. Nationally, some administrators just don't understand the principle need for communication. But we forgive them.

The vast majority of our instructors, however, did represent and demand excellence. In order to do so, they withstood grief from all of us. Some of them are forced to worry about layoff notices or to fight aggressively to protect the caliber of their programs. Most are characterized by an unparalleled dedication to their students.

I would like to express our gratitude to all of the teachers who have helped to mold us over the years; to the counselors and support staff who have helped us through the rough times and shuffled our college applications; to the administrators who have worked to provide a positive atmosphere. As the Swiss psychiatrist Carl Jung said, "One looks back with appreciation to the brilliant teachers, but with gratitude to those who touched our human feelings. The curriculum is so much necessary raw material, but warmth is the vital element for the growing plant and for the soul of the child."

In general, my teachers have truly inspired in me a desire for continual and eternal learning. That, to me, is the goal of high school. Many of us have already forgotten how to graph $f(t)=5t^2 + t + 1$ using polar coordinates. Some might feign amnesia when it comes to gas laws or acid-base chemistry or cannot recollect in what century the War of

1812 occurred. Others have disremembered the location of the Aegean Sea or have chosen to forget Ohm's law.

But if you are leaving high school with a true desire to continue learning, for the sake of learning, then the school has succeeded in its mission. If you are leaving only with the desire to get your bachelor's degree and distance yourself from scholarship as soon as possible, then a tragedy has occurred.

Although the new graduation process at Burnsville High was faster, it didn't quite have the glamour of the traditional graduation ceremony.

To explain it in this Common Sense manner, by rewriting a quotation of Thomas Paine, "The summer scholar and the sunshine pupil will, in this defining time, shrink from the service of his self; but he or she that actively engages in learning now, will reap the fruits of his or her labors."

I would also like to pay tribute to our families, who have believed in us, supported us, strengthened us as individuals.

As the sun prepares to set on our high school education, and our diplomas promise to proudly adorn the wall, I would like to thank every one of you for sharing this occasion with me. To thank my classmates, those of you with whom I have interacted daily, for eighteen years or just one. Those of you whom I wish I had gotten to know better.

But life is all about transition. Someone whose life lacks change is inevitably in a coma. We, on the other hand, are very much alive. And so, the future looms ahead, just like an Advanced Placement test or a final examination.

Recognizing that you cannot rehearse for life, I would like to wish you all the best, as you change carousels on the ride of life. I hope that all of you guys and dolls will find your dreamcoat as your quest for a Technicolor secret garden crescendos. I hope that you find your equilibrium and that you grow exponentially as a human being. I hope that you always have the writing device of your choice, be it crayon or computer.

I hope that your every angle will prove complementary.

Lastly, as our parole beckons, I am confident that "our future's so bright we've got to wear shades" as we are "cruising to a victory."

Thank you.

◆ Scott Wilcox

It's over. That's it. No more High School. No more bastard father constantly breathing down my neck. I don't need a sense of closure. I'm so ready to leave. I have a sense of closure: I'm finishing in the top 10 percent and I never killed my father! My two great accomplishments! I've had fun and I'll always remember my High School years fondly, but not with the same wistfulness as other people. Most of the people that I can share inside jokes with are already gone anyway. Now it's my turn to leave; I feel like I'm busting out into the great wide world of experiences. I see a whole horizon of possibilities opening up to me in college and after college.

In a way I'm scared of leaving, just because I don't want to disappoint myself. What if I just become a housewife and never fulfill any of my dreams? I don't want to risk my future, but nor do I want to limit the present. I have to find the Happy Medium. Always be conscientious, but never lose my spontaneity and self-assurance. I know this life is all I have, and I don't want to squander a second of it. The only problem I have now is that I don't know what to do with it. It's like when you save everything in case you'll ever use it, but never do. I'm afraid that is what my life will become. I'll be so afraid of wasting it that I'll never use it. So I should just go with the flow, and never get too caught up in what I want to become, just concentrate on what I am. And never be afraid of changing.

I feel like my life is just beginning—I feel this overwhelming sense of freedom. I have so much ahead of me and it's all mine for the making. Now I can decide what I want to do and do it. If I decide to live in a dirty house, well then, I just *will!* If I decide to come home drunk at

3:00 A.M. and accept the consequences, that is exactly what I will do. Having control over my life is very important to me. I never want to put my life into anybody else's hands again. Everything I do will be because I chose to do it. I *love* that thought. My life is my own!

◆ *Isabelle Evans*

Today is the first day of the rest of your life.

◆ *Abbie Hoffman*

It's scary to think that I'll be out on my own in the real world very soon. I am just a kid trying to survive in high school, get good grades, have fun and still be a gentleman. I've got problems just like the next person, and I don't expect all my questions to be answered. But lately I've started looking at myself more, and caring more about the man I am becoming. I realize that I've made mistakes, hurt people, lied and acted in a horrid manner to the people I love. I can only say, "I'm sorry, but I'm still growing up."

◆ *Richard Laurence*

Every exit is an entry somewhere else.

◆ *Tom Stoppard*

NO HURRY

As I stand here in front of you, I am going to say the one thing that you would never expect to come out of the mouth of a graduating senior.

I'm in no hurry to leave.

I like it that my mom makes my dinner, the laundry mysteriously gets cleaned, and the phone bill isn't my responsibility.

I have always taken comfort in my life's predictability. I have always known what school I was attending in the fall, what teachers I would have, and all the kids in my class.

It really is those little things you take for granted in such a small town that you realize are part of who you are. I love the fact that I can tell you how to get around all of Dixon without ever using street names, and on top of that, knowing that if I left my house, nine times out of ten I would see someone who has known me my whole life.

You could almost say that I'm scared to leave. But it is a different fear than I have ever experienced. It is not like being stuck in the dark when you're little, or like that time you watched *Friday the 13th* at two in the morning with your best friend. The fear itself is laced with the excitement you get when you're on a first date: you know it will turn out great but you still get nervous.

Circling memories and emotions, all of it. As I stand here I can almost feel the cool air lifting off the grass of the football field on one of those many Friday nights we spent here watching the game. The rush of the excitement of the impending summer. The smell of the pavement in the rain and the masses of people squished together in the hall at break trying not to get wet.

Everyone I have talked to over the past couple of weeks cannot stop talking about getting out of here and leaving for good, but I know at one point or another they will look back and miss Dixon a little. Life does not always offer teachers to help you out and in my case build self-confidence, but the lessons of life you have learned here will take you far.

I am in no hurry to leave.

Then again, I am in no hurry to stay. I am personally looking forward to living in a town with a movie theater and more than one stoplight. But even with all its downfalls, nowhere else will ever be home to me. Nothing will replace our memories; those we will take with us.

Maybe, just maybe, we are not as much on our own as I first thought. A part of me will always remain in the halls of Dixon High.

When I was a child, I thought as a child, and when I knew better, my thoughts grew too.

I am in no hurry to leave.

I know where I have been and I do not know where we are all going, but being here right now with all of you is most important.

◆ *Emily Browning*

Each that we lose takes part of us;
A crescent still abides,
Which like the moon, some turbid night,
Is summoned by the tides.

◆ *Emily Dickinson*

I try to learn from the past, but I plan for the future by focusing exclusively on the present. That's where the fun is.

◆ *Donald Trump*

When the details of the last four years are blurred by current events, I'll recall the moments someone took me aside to see how I was "really doing," or the sly, mischievous smiles exchanged with a friend sharing a private joke. I will remember the phone calls when I'd been away from a friend who wanted to hear my voice, or the private notes to remind me I'm special and appreciated. I'll be able to feel the casual arm around my shoulder or the easy companionship of a friend who knew I needed to talk. My mind will recall the sound of my mother's encouraging voice, believing I could achieve anything, and I'll remember the smiles of encouragement from friends who wanted my success. I'll see the faces of people who might have remained strangers had they not made the effort to make my acquaintance. Even the smile someone offered in passing or the person who never neglected to say "hello" will remain with me.

These gestures are simple, as is the message I have to share with you tonight, but more often than not, simple has the most profound impact. Each one of us has the opportunity to begin a new stage in our lives by building upon the experiences of the past and our hopes for the future. George Washington Carver wisely said, "How far you go in life depends on your being tender with the young, compassionate with the aged, sympathetic with the striving, and tolerant of the weak and strong—because someday you will have been all of these." His words touch me deeply because they remind me of the impact we have on our own lives through love. We can decide now who we will be. No matter where the future leads, there is the potential within all of us to put our lives into perspective and strive to make the greatest impact we can possibly make—through gestures of love.

◆ *Mindy May*

Tomorrow hopes we have learned something from yesterday.

◆ *John Wayne*

COMMENCEMENT

I remember graduation,
and my foolish thoughts that day. . . .
How I wished that I could skip it,
and get on about my way!

Plans for celebrating elsewhere
were my only real concern.
Thinking "education's over" . . .
spare me platform and lectern!

Organ music piped us in
with sounds of "Pomp and Circumstance,"
Alma Mater, Go Forth speeches,
boring all into a trance.

Then we marched across the stage
and shook a hand and grabbed a "scroll."
Was this simulated sheepskin
worth the trouble of this droll?

Smugly walking back towards
our seats, we passed our kith and kin.
It was then I saw a sight
that stirred my young adrenaline.

Here and there I spotted teachers
that I'd had along the way;
they had come, not from requirement,
but to honor us that day.

Mom and Dad were hand-in-hand,
and watched me as I passed them by. . . .
Mother's eyes were full of tears,
and Daddy held his proud head high.

Uncle Keith sat right beside him,
next was dearest Aunt Jo Ann,
then I realized my folly
as I stole a glance at them. . . .

Graduation exercises
aren't for us, the senior class.
Look around . . . the ones who love us
now enfold us, as we pass.

How could we have been so selfish
not to realize this day
called Commencement Exercises
marks the end of naïveté.

This day isn't for the students . . .
it's for those that carried us
to this point of our berated . . .
"Academic Exodus."

As the recessional began,
I had them once again in view.
Silently, with glistening cheeks,
I mouthed the heartfelt words "Thank you . . ."

◆ *Henry Matthew Ward*

There will come a time when you believe everything is finished. That will be the beginning.

◆ *Louis L'Amour*

This is one of those rare moments
　　　of life when you find yourself looking
　　　back on where you have been, while
　　　at the same time looking forward to
　　　the future.

Behind you are precious memories of
　　　experiences that you will never forget,
　　　heartfelt emotions that will fade but never disappear,
　　　and ideals that will change in form but remain in substance.

Ahead of you are new challenges and goals.
　　　They may seem mere shadows today,
　　　but they will one day be central to your life.

It seems such a paradox to look backward
　　　and forward at once, but the significance of any
　　　achievement exists in that very contradiction.
　　　Without your past, you have nothing on which to build your
　　　future.
　　　Without the future, your past would have no
　　　opportunity to come into full bloom.

◆ *Pamela Koehlinger*

THE PEOPLE WHO MADE IT POSSIBLE

◆ ◆ ◆

◆　◆　◆

TEACHERS

In a completely rational society, the best of us would aspire to be teachers and the rest of us would have to settle for something less, because passing civilization along from one generation to the next ought to be the highest honor and the highest responsibility anyone could have.

◆ *Lee Iacocca*

It is the supreme art of the teacher to awaken joy in creative expression and knowledge.

◆ *Albert Einstein*

Most of the kids in my class wanted to entertain each other, but my goal was to amuse the adults. I was the teacher's pet because I could make the teachers laugh.

◆ *Rosie O'Donnell*

Teaching is not always about passing on what you know, it is about passing on who you are.

◆ *Julia Loggins*

The mediocre teacher tells. The good teacher explains. The superior teacher demonstrates. The great teacher inspires.

William A. Ward

For some unimaginable reason, a handful of my teachers didn't give up on me as a hopeless moron. . . . My English teacher, Mrs. Hawkes, urged me to take her creative writing class. I figured, "What the hell, sounds easy!" But it wasn't—at first, anyway. One day, after class, she took me aside and said, "You know, I always hear you telling funny stories to your friends in class. You should write down some of those stories and we can make that your homework assignment." Hey, it sounded better than poetry!

So I gave it a try and—amazingly . . . I actually enjoyed it. I'd spend hours writing a story (usually about something stupid that happened at school), reading it to myself, crossing out things that weren't funny. I'd do four or five drafts, then hand it in. Suddenly, it was fun to go to class and stand up to read my funny story—and, best of all, to get some laughs. I was always grateful to Mrs. Hawkes for that.

Jay Leno

Wanting to teach is like wanting to have children or to write or paint or dance or invent or think through a mathematical problem that only a few have been able to solve. It has an element of mystery, involving as it does the yearly encounter with new people, the fear that you will be inadequate to meeting their needs, as well as the rewards of seeing them become stronger because of your work. And as is true of the other creative challenges, the desire to teach and the ability to teach well are not the same thing. With the rarest of exceptions, one has to learn how to become a good teacher just as one has to become a scientist or artist.

◆ *Herbert Kohl*

In teaching, the greatest sin is to be boring.

◆ *Johann Friedrich Herbart*

It's the last class of the day, and we're rolling. Suddenly there's an annoying knock on the door. I open it and find a tall, attractive black woman standing there. She looks too young to be someone's mother. "Can I help you?" I ask, trying to conceal my irritation at the interruption.

Then it hits me. It's Lettie Moses, Class of '78—but she's taller and slimmer than I'd remembered. She's graduated from Smith College and is on her way to the University of Michigan Law School. Lettie, from the Alexandria housing projects. Lettie, whose loving mother and father were determined to see her succeed.

"I just dropped by to say hello," she says.

We talk in the hall for a few minutes, catching up on four years of news. Her visit makes my day. I think what she really was saying to me was "I just wanted to let you know I made it." And I was thinking, Lettie, I know you would have made it without me, but just being a tiny part of your growth and success, just witnessing it, that's what teaching is all about.

◆ *Patrick Welsh*

Teachers are sort of faced with a thankless task, because no matter how good they are, unless they find a way to personally rationalize the rewards of their effort, nobody else is really going to do it for them en masse.

I think it's so important for the students to give teachers feedback. Say, "I really appreciate what you're doing, and what you're doing is good. You've helped me, you've really changed my life. You really make a difference in my life."

◆ *Julius Erving*

I always think we live, spiritually, by what others have given us in the significant hours of our life. These significant hours do not announce themselves as coming, but arrive unexpected. Nor do they make a great show of themselves; they pass almost unperceived. Often, indeed, their significance comes home to us first as we look back, just as the beauty of a piece of music or of a landscape often strikes us first in our recollection of it. Much that has become our own in gentleness, modesty, kindness, willingness to forgive, in veracity, loyalty, resignation under suffering, we owe to people in whom we have seen or experienced these virtues at work, sometimes in a great matter, sometimes in a small. A thought which had become act sprang into us like a spark, and lighted a new flame within us.

◆ *Albert Schweitzer*

A teacher affects eternity; he can never tell where his influence stops.

◆ *Henry Adams*

There were three or four teachers along the way that inspired me. I wasn't particularly good in English — I didn't really like it that much — but I had a high school English teacher who was just brilliant.

I don't know whether he taught me very much, but he certainly inspired me to be creative and try to write things. And when you think about your best teachers, they are people that you look up to and are inspired by more than people who actually got the concepts across to you.

George Lucas

One looks back with appreciation to the brilliant teachers, but with gratitude to those who touched our human feelings. The curriculum is so much necessary raw material, but warmth is the vital element for the growing plant and for the soul of the child.

Carl Jung

I had the benefit of some very good high school English teachers. One in particular when I was a senior in high school. I was a jock, okay. I was not a student. Although I enjoyed reading, that was about it as far as academics. But she forced us to read good books and good writers, particularly good American writers. [Her name is] Francis McGuffey. She's still teaching, and we still correspond. She comes to my book signings in Memphis when I'm there. I send her an autographed copy of every book. We're still friends, still buddies.

John Grisham

In the fourth grade, Mrs. Duncan was my greatest inspiration. In the fourth grade was when I first, I think, began to believe in myself. For the first time I believed I could do almost anything. . . . I was so inspired. And a lot of it was because of Mrs. Duncan, Mrs. Duncan, Mrs. Duncan. We did a show not too long ago, and I had favorite teachers on, I just broke down. First of all, it was the first time that I realized that Mrs. Duncan had a name other than Mrs. Duncan. You know, your teachers never have names. I said, sobbing, "Her name's Mary!" I couldn't believe it.

◆ *Oprah Winfrey*

I do not believe that we can put into anyone ideas which are not in him already. As a rule there are in everyone all sorts of good ideas, ready like tinder. But much of this tinder catches fire, or catches it successfully, only when it meets some flame or spark from outside, i.e., from some other person. Often, too, our own light goes out, and is rekindled by some experience we go through with a fellow man. Thus we have each of us cause to think with deep gratitude of those who have lighted the flames within us.

◆ *Albert Schweitzer*

When I was asked by this senior class to speak at Baccalaureate, I was very surprised that after listening to me speak to you in the classroom for the last four years, you'd actually want to hear me speak again! It occurred to me in that moment that perhaps the greater part of love is listening to someone, and finding what they say to be valuable. I want to thank you for your listening, and I feel very honored to be here.

I am going to go against the grain of almost every graduation and baccalaureate speech in the world tonight and *not* speak to you about your future. And let me tell you why—because in truth, there is only one thing your future holds for sure, and that is death.

Let me back up for a second. When you ask most teachers why they went into education, they will tell you about a teacher they had in the past who inspired them or cared for them or who believed in them and made a difference. Well, I'm one of the exceptions to the rule—I can't remember having any teacher like that, and probably became a teacher *in spite* of what they did, rather than *because* of it.

But I have had several great teachers in life, and one of them is death. From death I have learned some powerful lessons that I'd like to share with you tonight. And though death has touched my life in a multitude of ways, there are three stories that I want to share to begin with.

The first is about the time when I was twelve or thirteen years old. I used to house-sit for my next-door neighbors, Linda and Bob, when they went away on vacation. Well, I've always been an intensely curious person, and my curiosity took the form in those days of being a great snoop! And, I liked to have a partner to snoop with, so one day I invited my good buddy Brian Meyers over to snoop with me. We had a great time going through Linda and Bob's closet, through their cabinets, and we finally ended up in their bedroom. I sat down on the bed and opened up a drawer by the head of the bed. I saw Brian's eyes get big, as he reached down and picked up something in the drawer—a gun. He wrapped his hand around the gun, put his finger on the trigger, and in slow motion brought the head of the barrel up and placed it against my forehead, and pulled the trigger. The gun went off loudly, and I felt the pressure of the shot and fell back on the bed, waiting—and hoping—to go to heaven.

After a few minutes without angelic intervention, I opened my eyes, and realized that heaven looked an awful lot like Linda and Bob's ceiling! I reached my hand up to my forehead to where I felt the gunshot, and to my surprise could find no hole. I sat up and saw poor Brian, white as a ghost and scared to death. We thought maybe the bullet had bounced off my hard head and gone through a wall somewhere, and we ran around trying to find it, but couldn't. It was then that I learned about guns that shoot blanks. Ever since then I feel like I am here on borrowed time, here because, by the grace of God, Linda and Bob have a gun that shoots blanks by their bed instead of a gun that shoots bullets. A single thoughtless act showed me the absolute precariousness of life, and the ease of how it can transition, completely senselessly, into death.

Another lesson taught to me by death occurred many years later, when I was in college. A friend of mine who was two years younger than I had just graduated from high school, and one day we met in early August for lunch. Her name was Donetta, and she was the kindest, smartest, most loving person I knew. We talked about what we had been doing over the summer, and she shared with me how miserable she was. She had broken up with her high school boyfriend and hadn't seen any of her friends since graduation. She felt like she was losing everybody she cared about, but she had one hope. At the end of the month, she was going off to college. She shared with me how glad she would be to leave, to get out of the small town, and meet new friends and start new relationships. She felt like she was wilting that summer, and needed to be transplanted.

Two days after that lunch, I found out she was killed by an eighteen-wheeler that ran a stop light when she was passing through the intersection in her small car.

A third lesson I learned from death was from a story my good friend Karen shared with me. She and her fiancé were living together, and on the night of their second anniversary they had planned a special dinner to discuss their wedding arrangements. He came home from work in a bad mood, and they started a fight about something petty, and the fight escalated until he stormed out of the house angrily. She was angry too for a while, but as the night went on she forgave him, and decided to make him the special dinner as planned and have it waiting for him when he came home. Hours passed, and it got later and later and later, until there was a knock on the door. She ran to open it, thinking it was him, only to find the police there. Her fiancé had stopped by a convenience store and was shot to death in his car in a completely random act of violence.

So this is why I say to you that I can't speak to you in good faith about your future, because none of us are sure we'll even have one. From the three stories that I've shared with you now, and many more in the meantime, I have learned that life is absolutely precious, and can be taken away from us without warning or preparation.

Now, I tell you these stories, at the risk of seeming morbid, because death has so much to teach us about life. It teaches us that we don't have a future, and in teaching us that, it actually teaches us something more important—to value every moment of the present.

If Donetta had been focused on the present, if she knew she would

Charlene soon began to realize that being the teacher's pet wasn't all it was cracked up to be.

never live to go to college, you and I both know her summer would have been a very different one, as she would have made the most out of her last remaining days. If Karen had been focused on the present, and known that her fiancé would not come back that night after their fight, you and I both know she would never have let him walk out that door angry.

I use those lessons in my everyday life all the time, and I give them to you tonight to use in yours, if you haven't experienced death first-hand. I ask myself often, If today were my last day alive, would I have lived it and loved it fully? And, unless there's a faculty meeting that day, the answer is almost always yes! I ask myself often, Is there anyone in my life who, if they died today, I would feel regret at not saying something to them? A woman named Angeles Arrien wrote, "The greatest remorse is love unexpressed," so I ask myself if there's anyone I haven't expressed my love to fully, and if there is, I do so. If I find myself getting too focused on the future at the expense of the present, I stop myself and find the beauty and joy in being alive now. Those are some of the most powerful, life-altering lessons I've learned from one of my greatest teachers: death.

You know, time is a funny thing. In Western culture we tend to think of time as a straight line, with the past moving into the present and into the future, similar to a time line. In this approach, you're always driven to get somewhere, to move along the line, and the goal is always the future. And how we measure movement of time is by milestones—or what we know in our culture today as "Kodak moments." You're having one now by the way, so pay attention!

It starts with our parents, who often buy those baby books to mark these moments for us. Our first smile. Our first tooth. Our first step. Our first word. Our first day of school. Our first dance. Our eighth-grade graduation. Now, your baccalaureate. And on Saturday, your high school graduation. But if you take all these milestones and add up the amount of time they actually take, it's really minuscule. By the time you graduate from high school, you have lived over 6,000 days, and maybe 15 or 20 of them were these milestone events. That's why they're called Kodak moments—because they go by as quickly as a flash of a camera. And seniors, I've got news for you—it doesn't get any better—in fact, as you grow up, you have fewer of those moments. Maybe your first day of college. Maybe graduating from college. Maybe your first "real" job. Maybe your wedding day. Maybe the birth of your children. And then you turn over your scrapbook to them, and start keeping track of their milestones. Their first smile. Their first tooth. Their first step. And so on.

And on our grand time line, we string all these Kodak moments together in a scrapbook and call them a life. But I assert that life is not what's recorded there—symbols of life are. Your high school graduation photo and diploma are not a measure of how successfully educated you are—what you do with that education after graduation is. Your wedding day photo is not a measure of how successfully you love—how you treat your spouse every day after your wedding is. A picture of you holding your newborn baby is not a measure of how successful a parent you are—how you raise that baby and love that baby for the rest of his or her life is.

So it seems to me a mistake to focus on the future and on these great milestone events in the future as a way of defining success and happiness. It seems to me that defining time as a line linking the past to the present to the future is a mistaken way of viewing it. You see, the past can't become the future—the future actually becomes the past. Think about it. You are moving towards this thing called graduation on Saturday, and it's in the future. But the minute you get there, it becomes the past. You'll march in to sit down, and the marching becomes the past. Someone will give a speech, and the speech becomes the past. You'll be handed your diploma, and you'll leave the field and you'll go back to your house for a party, and then all of graduation, which was this grand future you planned for, is now the past, gone as fast as a flash of a camera. And how does the future move into the past? Through the present. The future moves through the present and becomes the past, and then the next moment in the future moves through the present and becomes the past, and thus it seems to me that time is really more appropriately conceived of as a circle rather than a line.

Now the beauty of the model of the circle is that there is no longer a destination—a point on the line to get to—but life becomes meaningful in the journey itself, in the flowing of time itself, not in some imaginary end that will make it all worthwhile. And if life is focused on the journey rather than the destination, our focus moves away from the future and into the rightful place, the present.

So given that all we have is the present, and that life is about the journey and not the destination, then how do we make the journey one of joy and happiness? For as Maya Angelou expressed so beautifully, "It is in the search itself that one finds the ecstasy." I want to pass on to you now what I've learned about living the ecstatic life.

A very wise man named Richard Baker Roshi once said, "All we have in life is what we notice." Really, if you think about it, it's true. We only really own in life what we notice. For example, if you're walking down the hallway at school and you notice your boyfriend noticing another girl, you may get upset. However, you are really only upset because you *noticed* him noticing. If he noticed on the sly, you couldn't be upset, because you wouldn't even know it happened! Or, another example. Maybe you are walking down the street and notice ten dollars on the sidewalk, and you pick it up and put it in your wallet and are really happy. The only reason you are happy is because you *noticed* the money. If you walked down the sidewalk and didn't notice it, you couldn't be happy about it!

See, your emotions are driven by what you notice. How you experience life is driven by what you notice. And, more than that, your happiness is driven by what you *focus* on when you notice something. Let me explain that.

Last month I took my honors class to this park to write a poem about what they noticed in nature. I told them very clearly that they should sit by themselves and write for the whole period. But when I looked over off in the distance, I could see three of my boys at the baseball diamond, one playing catcher, one playing pitcher, one playing batter, with an imaginary ball and bat.

Now, the first thing I noticed was that they weren't doing the assignment—they weren't doing what I told them to do, and I felt a flash of anger. But then, I noticed something else. One of them threw an imaginary pitch, and one of them hit the imaginary ball out into left field, and ran around the bases, scoring an imaginary home run, while the other one tried to field the imaginary ball and get the runner out. And I noticed how much fun they were having, and how they looked just like five-year-old boys playing out there. And I noticed that these same boys who walk the hallways every day trying consciously to look very cool were unconsciously looking *not* cool in the most charming of ways. All of a sudden I felt such joy—when I focused on what they *were* doing instead of what they *weren't* doing.

So I think that's a key to being happy in the present. Not to notice what's wrong, but to notice what's right. Have you ever noticed that you mostly notice what's wrong? For example, have you ever noticed that you never notice your feet unless something's wrong with them? You walk around on them all the time, but you don't notice them unless your shoes are too tight, or your feet ache, or you have a blister. You never notice your stomach unless it hurts or you are hungry. If a car cuts you off on the freeway on your way to work, it can put you in a bad mood, but what you failed to notice was the two hundred other cars on the freeway who stayed in their own lanes, which should put you in a good mood!

You know, I tried this out on my friend Paul recently. He had hurt his arm quite badly in a skiing accident, and every week when we got together for class, all our classmates would always ask him how his arm was. And it really put him in a bad mood, because it would call more attention to what was wrong with him, and where he hurt. So I took the opposite approach. Whenever I would see him, I would say, "Hey, Paul, how are your legs?" or "Hey, Paul, how's your stomach doing?" And invariably his face would light up and he would smile and say, "Just fine, now that I think about it!"

Now, I have a theory for why we always notice what's wrong. It's because there's a lot less of it. Really. What's wrong stands out because there's so much right. See, the brain can only process so much information. For example, if you have a cut on one finger, you notice that rather than the other nine because there's only one of them to notice.

If you've ever noticed, the function of the news is to point out what's wrong. I've noticed something in the news lately—it seems like every day in Sacramento some man is killing his wife. This really upsets me to see. But imagine, every day in Sacramento 300,000 men come home from work and *don't* kill their wives. Can you imagine that on the news? "Tonight, John Smith came home from work and didn't kill his wife again. Highlights at eleven." You see, that's not news. If your only contact with the world was by watching the news, you'd think this world was the most horrible place ever. It's not. It's actually a great place 99 percent of the time, but the role of the news in this country is to notice what's wrong, not what's right. That's why I rarely watch the news, because I know that my happiness is directly connected to what I notice, and I don't want to notice what's wrong all the time.

So here's the trick, the ultimate key to living an ecstatic life. *The key to having a great life is noticing how great the life you're having is.* If you want a more joyful life, notice more joy in your life. Surround yourself by people who are joyous. If you want a more loving life, notice more love in your life. Surround yourself by people who are loving. Better yet, become yourself more joyous, more loving, and then you'll notice other people noticing you!

This is important, because have you ever noticed how we even try to enroll people in noticing bad things? We'll say things like, "Did you notice what a jerk that guy just was?" "No, but now you point it out, he was"—and now you've got another jerk in your life! I think we should have a new national motto—"If you can't notice anything nice, don't notice anything at all." We should have a national "Notice Love" week. A national "Notice Cuteness" week. And while we're waiting for that to happen, I have a suggestion. Establish reflective practices, like writing in a journal, or meditation, or prayer, where you spend time reflecting on the good that you've noticed. Sit down at the dinner table at night and share the good that you've noticed with each other.

The Native Americans have a saying to remind themselves to notice the good, and I had it printed in your program for you, because it's very powerful. This particular wording is attributed to the Navajo, but I have seen other derivations of it, which leads me to believe that it may be universal wisdom in the Native American culture. It's said like this:

This that is beautiful, it shows my way;
This that is beautiful, it shows my way;
This that is beautiful, it shows my way;

before me, it is beautiful, it shows my way;
behind me, it is beautiful, it shows my way;
This that is beautiful, it shows my way.

As you say this, you turn in a circle and face each of the four directions. Please stand and join me in saying this.

Isn't that great? I think it should replace the Macarena as our next big craze! You see, to the Native Americans the circle is very sacred, and they acknowledge the beauty of everything in all four directions and in the past, present, and future in this one saying.

Now, I say all of this, and some of you chuckle and think, Yeah, right. We really love only certain parts of our lives, and miss the beauty of the rest. What a tragedy to spend all of high school for one moment: graduation. It's sometimes hard to see the day in, day out beauty of it all. This class is beautiful, it shows my way. This test is beautiful, it shows my way. This homework assignment is beautiful, it shows my way. I've watched you for four years, and I know you're more likely to say, Lunch is beautiful, it shows my way (outta here). The last bell of the day is beautiful, it shows my way (outta here). Summer vacation is beautiful, it shows my way (outta here). But when you do that, you are living for those brief moments in the future and missing the beauty of the present. You are living for the destination and missing the beauty, the ecstasy, of the journey.

And listen, I'm not blind to the fact that there's a lot of bad out there in the world. You might turn one direction and see a friend struggling with a drug problem. You might turn another direction and see a parent lose his or her job. You might turn another direction and witness an act of violence, or be a victim yourself. But don't miss the key part of the saying: "This that is beautiful—*it shows my way.*" Every time you turn a direction and see pain or suffering, your way is being shown. And the way being shown is always to love, because I truly

**Mrs. Mutner liked to go over a few of her rules
on the first day of school.**

believe that every problem in the world, when reduced to its simplest and most elementary form, is always a lack of love, a cry for love.

So I want to end by talking about love a little bit, but first, I want to visit the idea of heaven. One of the most intriguing passages in the Bible comes from the sixteenth chapter of the Book of Matthew. Jesus says, "I will give you the keys to the kingdom of heaven." Now listen up, you guys, this is good. "I will give you the keys to the kingdom of heaven; whatever you bind on earth will be bound in heaven, and whatever you loose on earth will be loosed in heaven." One way to interpret this is, for example, if you have a problem giving up money on earth, you will have a problem with giving in heaven. If you have a problem controlling your anger on earth, you will have a problem with it in heaven. Now that's a really scary thought on the one hand, and a very powerful one on the other. It's scary because it means that we take all of our stuff, all our baggage with us to heaven. But it's also powerful, because it means that what we want to create in heaven, we can create first on earth.

But first, we have to be present, because what Jesus is telling us is there is no magical place in the future where everything will be different, will get better. Heaven is not a milestone, or a Kodak moment. No one will be there to take pictures for you. This is me entering the Pearly Gates. This is me getting my angel wings. This is me standing with St. Peter and God. No, heaven is the present, and it is up to us to create it—right here, right now.

And ultimately, what do all of us want in heaven? Love. We dream of a place where, for twenty-four hours a day, the temperature will be the temperature we love. We think of angels playing the music we love. We dream of eating all the food we love. We dream of meeting up again with the people we love. We dream of being reunited with the God we love.

So this is the key to the kingdom of heaven on earth. Love. Vincent van Gogh said, "To know God, love many things." Deepak Chopra said, "Loving another person is not separate from loving God. One is a single wave, the other is the ocean." Tolstoy said, "Love is life. All, all that I understand I understand only because I love. Everything is, everything exists only because I love. All is connected by love alone. Love is God, and to die means that I, a particle of love, shall return to the universal and eternal source." Every major and minor religion has at its core love as its most important principle. Every great religious and spiritual leader, and a great many of our important secular ones, have had one major message—the power of love. They know the truth that will set us free: the only way to create heaven on earth is to love.

Is it easy to love people all of the time? No. Is it easy to love your life all of the time? No. Now, there's stuff we have to do in life that we don't want to do. Like I personally find it hard to love going to the dentist! It's hard for me to be present and love that. So I create a possibility of love around it. I say, I am going to the dentist so I can have fresh breath and nice teeth for my loved ones. And I lay there in the chair with the drill in my mouth and I think how much I must love people to want to have clean teeth and fresh breath for them!

I caught myself getting really irritated and not loving my life last week when I had to take my car in to get a smog check. I had already missed the deadline and had to pay the DMV some outrageous late fee, and I couldn't find a smog place without a line of five cars long, and I didn't have much time—you can imagine my frustration and displeasure! So I noticed that I wasn't enjoying the present very much, and I decided to shift my way of thinking about it from burden to love. And you know what, it wasn't very hard! I realized that getting my car smogged is all about loving the environment, loving our great Mother Nature, loving my fellow human beings enough to want to keep the air fresh and clean and breathable for them. So as I sat there waiting, I sat there waiting out of love. You can create the possibility of love out of any situation, and when you do it this way, things suddenly become not only bearable but enjoyable. Changing a dirty diaper is an act of love for your baby, showing how much you care for the baby's comfort. Taking a test is an act of love for your teacher, showing how much you have learned and appreciate the knowledge he or she provided. Filing papers for three hours at a secretarial job is an act of love for the clients, wanting their records to be in order in case they need to access them.

In fact, every job out there can be a manifestation of and a gift of love. Really, that's the only reason to do a job. If you want to be an actress, do it because you love the audience. If you want to be a politician, do it out of love for your constituents. If you want to be a mechanic, do it because you love making cars safe for people to drive. If you want to be a farmer, do it because you love the thought of providing people with food to sustain their lives. And for God's sake, if you want to be a teacher, do it because you love the kids.

I have spoken many words tonight, but my message is actually short, and simple. To the seniors, I want to tell you that I notice you. You are beautiful and strong, and for the last four years you have shown my way. Stay present to the beauty and the ecstasy of life, and treasure every step on the journey rather than focusing on the destination. Love everyone and everything, and express yourself with every ounce of the passion you possess. Do these things, and the keys to the kingdom of heaven on earth are yours, not in the future, but now.

Thank you for the love that you've given me by listening, and know that I love you all very much.

◆ *Jennifer Leigh Selig*

Teachers open the door, but you must enter by yourself.

◆ *Chinese Proverb*

Everyone who remembers his own educational experience remembers teachers, not methods and techniques. The teacher is the kingpin of the educational situation. He makes and breaks programs.

◆ *Sidney Hook*

FRIENDS

My best friend is the one who brings out the best in me.

◆ *Henry Ford*

Think where man's glory most begins and ends,
And say my glory was I had such friends.

◆ *William Butler Yeats*

Each friend represents a world in us, a world possibly not born until
they arrive, and it is only by this meeting that a new world is born.

◆ *Anaïs Nin*

True love is the gift which God hath given,
to man alone beneath the heaven. The
silver link, the silver tie, which heart
to heart, and mind to mind, in body
and in soul can bind.

◆ *Unknown*

Have I ever told you're my hero?
You're everything I would like to be.
I can climb higher than an eagle.
You are the wind beneath my wings.

◆ *Larry Henley and Jeff Silbar*

Never shall I forget the time I spent with you. Please continue to be my friend, as you will always find me yours.

♦ *Ludwig van Beethoven*

WHAT MAKES A FRIEND

In kindergarten your idea of a good friend was the person who let you have the red crayon when all that was left was the ugly black one.

In first grade your idea of a good friend was the person who went to the bathroom with you and held your hand as you walked through the scary halls.

In second grade your idea of a good friend was the person who helped you stand up to the class bully.

In third grade your idea of a good friend was the person who shared their lunch with you when you forgot yours on the bus.

In fourth grade your idea of a good friend was the person who was willing to switch square dancing partners in gym so you wouldn't have to be stuck do-si-do-ing with Nasty Nicky or Smelly Susan.

In fifth grade your idea of a good friend was the person who saved a seat on the back of the bus for you.

In sixth grade your idea of a good friend was the person who went up to Nick or Susan, your new crush, and asked them to dance with you, so that if they said no you wouldn't have to be embarrassed.

In seventh grade your idea of a good friend was the person who let you copy the social studies homework from the night before that you had forgotten about.

In eighth grade your idea of a good friend was the person who helped you pack up your stuffed animals and old baseball cards so that your room would be a "high schooler's" room, but didn't laugh at you when you finished and broke out into tears.

In ninth grade your idea of a good friend was the person who went with you to that "cool" party thrown by a senior so you wouldn't wind up being the only freshman there.

In tenth grade your idea of a good friend was the person who changed their schedule so you would have someone to sit with at lunch.

In eleventh grade your idea of a good friend was the person who gave you rides in their new car, convinced your parents that you shouldn't be grounded, consoled you when you broke up with Nick or Susan, and found you a date to the prom.

In twelfth grade your idea of a good friend was the person who helped you pick out a college, assured you that you would get into that college, helped you deal with your parents, who were having a hard time adjusting to the idea of letting you go. . .

At graduation your idea of a good friend was the person who was crying on the inside but managed the biggest smile one could give as they congratulated you.

The summer after twelfth grade your idea of a good friend was the person who helped you clean up the bottles from that party, helped you sneak out of the house when you just couldn't deal with your parents, assured you that now that you and Nick or you and Susan were back together, you could make it through anything, helped you pack up for college and just silently hugged you as you looked through blurry eyes at eighteen years of memories you were leaving behind, and finally on those last days of childhood, went out of their way to come over and send you off with a hug, a lot of memories, reassurance that you would make it in college as well as you had these past eighteen years, and, most important, sent you off to college knowing you were loved.

Now, your idea of a good friend is still the person who gives you the better of the two choices, holds your hand when you're scared, helps you fight off those who try to take advantage of you, thinks of you at times when you are not there, reminds you of what you have forgotten, helps you put the past behind you but understands when you need to hold on to it a little longer, stays with you so that you have confidence, goes out of their way to make time for you, helps you clear up your mistakes, helps you deal with pressure from others, smiles for you when even they are sad, helps you become a better person, and, most important, loves you!

◆ *Author unknown*

Friends are the sunshine of life.

◆ *John Hay*

SEPARATE WAYS
for Maggie Stewart

As we separate tonight,
I don't feel the same,
It's just not right.

We will go our separate ways,
And I want to say so much,
But I realize I only have a few days.

Our friendship meant the world to me,
You gave me hope,
If only we could still be.

You were there morning, day, & night.
If only I could show you,
You were my light.

I will miss you,
Reach for the stars,
& I hope you find another friendship as good as ours.

◆ *Colleen Clyder*

Friendship is Love without his wings!

◆ *Lord Byron*

I cherish my friends, for I know that of all things granted us. . . none is greater or better than friendship.

Pietro Aretino

The richest man in the world is not the one who still has the first dollar he has ever earned. It's the man who still has his best friend.

Martha Mason

The real test of friendship is: Can you literally do nothing with the other person? Can you enjoy together those moments of life that are utterly simple? They are the moments people look back on at the end of life and number as their most sacred experiences.

Eugene Kennedy

It is one of the blessings of old friends that you can afford to be stupid with them.

Ralph Waldo Emerson

ONE PICTURE IN A YEARBOOK

One picture in a yearbook
black and white and small
of you, who loomed so colorful
and large in my life
for four years.

One picture in a yearbook
gazed upon so often
and with such longing,
the way I looked at you
though you never noticed.

One picture in a yearbook
a visual memory
a sacred image
all that remains of you
since we graduated
and went our separate ways.

One picture in a yearbook
to remember you by
many regrets of all the days
when we walked the same hallways
and I never told you how I felt.

Then your smile was three-dimensional
and my life was vivid color.

◆ *Alexandria Miller*

Old friends are the great blessing of one's later years. . . . They have a
memory of the same events and have the same mode of thinking.

◆ *Horace Walpole*

What is a friend? A single soul dwelling in two bodies.

Aristotle

FOREVER BEST FRIENDS

It seems to me as years have passed by,
There is one thing that we can't deny.
The friends that we've made will always remain.
Not one of us lost but all of us gained.

They have touched our souls and brightened our days,
brought smiles to our faces and changed our bad ways.
They've made us who we are, today and in the past.
We all look back now and wish those years hadn't gone so fast.

Remember walking down the halls we walk along no more
and seeing our friends' faces greeting us at the door.
We've laughed and we've cried throughout all the years.
We've made many strong bonds and overcome fears.

Our triumphs have been made, our victories have been sought.
Our defeats have been witnessed and tears have been brought.
We've faced our challenges as a group, and never as one.
A new challenge faces us today, another journey has begun.

The journey starts by moving on and always being brave.
What we kept is lost, but what we had we gave.
Moving on by ourselves without the friends we know.
It may be hard at first but forward we must go.

We all have our wants, our wishes, and dreams.
We've all built our friendships and sewn our own seams.
As we walk down the road of life we go a different way.
But maybe by fate or chance, we'll meet again someday.

The joys and happiness we've shared, it is so very true.
Promise me this—you'll remember me and I'll remember you.
Our time together is growing short, and we'll be apart,
but days and months and years from now you'll all be in my heart.

So I tell you, look to the future, but always remember the past.
Love your family and your friends and live like each day is your last.
This graduating class will somehow always be together.
In our minds and in our hearts we'll be remembered forever.

I wish you all love and I'll never forget,
that these years have gone by without one regret.
This chapter in our lives is coming to an end.
But all of us will truly be forever best friends.

Rosin Bergdoll

Friends are relatives you make for yourself.

♦ Eustache Deschamps

Your wealth is where your friends are.

♦ Plautus

My mom always said in life it is the little things that truly matter; perhaps I thought it to be true the first time she told me, but it was not until I was in love that I knew what she meant. He could give me the sun, the moon, and all the stars in the sky, but they probably would not mean as much as him just holding my hand or smiling at me from across the room. He could bring me a dozen roses or a silver necklace with his heart and they would not mean as much as the look on his face when he gives them to me. No company can package and sell his smile, write about it in a Hallmark card, or even put a pink box on all the little things in life he does.

All little girls grow up with ideas and images of what love is, but they never have their own; it is what they see others do, what they read about or watch on television. And this held true for me. . . . For a long time I did not believe in love or even think there was such a thing. Having parents who divorced when I was very young and seeing them go from one person to the next like children picking out candy, can and does give one, especially a little girl of six, some very false illusions of love. I thought love was something that only happened in the movies and would never happen to me. I felt like that for a very long time, through insufficient relationships from kindergarten through elementary school and on to junior high, when relationships were about chasing after one another on the playground and saying you were going out when the only place you were headed was the lunch line.

That was, until I saw him. . . . For the first time all over again.

It is very funny how you can go through elementary school, junior high, and even part of high school knowing a person's name and who they are without truly knowing them or how much they could affect and change your life in so many ways. He was supposedly in my fifth-grade class, but I do not remember his face smiling at me. We probably passed each other in the halls at least once a day in junior high, but I do not remember his hand reaching for mine. We sat next to each other in classes, but again I do not remember him whispering sweet jests into my ear. However, I do remember seeing his smile, his eyes, feeling his hand, and hearing his voice for the first time all over again last year—our junior year.

People often ask how we got together or who helped us get together, and for us I can say with a semi-smirk that Mark Twain did. It is funny how your name can be right by someone's in the alphabet without you even knowing it until you are in a group doing an English project on Mark Twain. Both of us went over to our other group member's house with no idea that this project would lead to so much more. I remember leaving her house with a new view on life and at least a dozen butterflies in my stomach, and then I was hit with one of the lowest parts of anybody's life: denial. He could not possibly like me, I am not good enough for him, he still yearns for someone else. . . . So you go on living your life, until you find out the other girl in your group has the same feelings for him! Of course it is a great lunchtime topic between the two of you—how perfect his smile is and how his shyness is so sweet—but secretly you have no choice but to be offended that she shares your personal feelings, and you ask yourself over and over again how she could possibly notice the same things you do, and you tell yourself it really shouldn't matter because you noticed him first!

Yes, then the roller-coaster ride begins when you find out he might possibly have the same feelings for you! You start going up to the top of the roller-coaster inch by inch, hearing every little chain movement, as you approach the top and head down towards embarrassment, upset, tears, smiles, happiness, more smiles, kisses, more tears, and love. And every time you approach the end of the coaster, you hope the attendant will give you one more free time around and are relieved to see yourself heading to the top again, knowing and not knowing what to expect, looking forward to the happy times and fearing the big dips down when the tears and pain come, but remembering you will always go up afterwards to the joy and love.

I remember the perfect moments we have shared together in each other's arms and underneath the stars. Every so often there is just one perfect kiss, in the cold night's air, when he brings me a rose after practice and his best friend is standing with his back to us, or as we hold each other when we are high up in the sky looking over one city and on the next one. Sometimes I wish every moment of our lives could be spent that way, but then I remember it would not be as special if it was always like that. I sometimes sit back and wonder what if our names were not right next to each other in the alphabet, or if we had not gone to our first movie together, or if he still had that infatuation for another and never gave me a chance. And I see my life as a very lonely life—sure I have my friends who I can go to when I need to and who can cheer me up when I am down—but my life would not be the same. I become totally scared at the thought of my life without him in it, and the role he plays. It reminds me every so often that I have to say to him, Thank you for being there and giving me the sun, the moon, the stars, your love, and my life with you.

◆ *Robanne Frederickson*

Wayne was deeply touched by the personal inscriptions in his yearbook.

I CAN'T LIVE WITHOUT HER

At the end of my sophomore year, I sat behind a girl named Robanne. All I knew about her was her name, she sat in front of me, and she was really nice (she helped me study for tests in class). The funny thing is, she had been there in our class since second grade. Never once before can I remember talking to her, or even getting to know her as a person.

That year ended with little more than an acquaintance. The next year much more was to come. We were in the same English class again, and this time the teacher assigned us to do an English assignment in a group of three. Here I was set up to work in a group with two girls, one I knew and the other I knew practically nothing about. The project we were assigned took us to the houses of our group partners. There I was able to get to know Robanne a little better. After a very short time I developed a crush on her. A little while later I heard from one of my friends that Robanne liked me, and wondered if I would say yes if she asked me to go on a date. I said I would.

When we went out on our first date, neither of us knew what to expect of each other. I picked her up at her house. Just like in the movies, her mom answered the door and then Robanne came down the stairs after her mom called her and we left. We went to the movies, and eventually we made it back to her house. The two of us sat in my truck for what seemed like hours, just sitting there, nobody saying a word. I was so nervous, not sure if she had a good time or what she was thinking. Finally I leaned over and kissed her. I don't know why I didn't do it sooner instead of sitting there like a jackass. After we kissed we said good night and she went inside. As I drove away I thought I had done everything wrong and that she was going to hate me. In the end, though, I guess I was wrong.

To this day, almost a year and six months from our first date, we are still together. It has become something far beyond a crush on a girl that you had when you were in elementary school. It has become something I love, someone I love. I have learned so much, experienced even more, and I love it all. I don't know what I would do right now if I didn't have Robanne, someone who a little over a year and a half ago I knew hardly anything about. I guess that is the only thing I can regret, that I should have acted sooner in getting to know her, because now I live to love her.

◆ *Johndavid Galindo*

There is nothing on this earth more to be prized than true friendship.

◆ *St. Thomas Aquinas*

Hold a true friend with both your hands.

◆ *Nigerian proverb*

NEW FRIENDS AND OLD FRIENDS

Make new friends, but keep the old;
Those are silver, these are gold.
New-made friendships, like new wine,
Age will mellow and refine.
Friendships that have stood the test—

Time and change—are surely best;
Brow may wrinkle, hair grow gray,

Friendship never knows decay.
For 'mid old friends, tried and true,
Once more we our youth renew.
But old friends, alas! may die,
new friends must their place supply.
Cherish friendship in your breast—
New is good, but old is best;
Make new friends, but keep the old;
Those are silver, these are gold.

◆ *Joseph Parry*

LOOKING BACK

Just looking back today,
On all the happy times we've known,
Thinking of our friendship,
And the way that it has grown.
I feel fortunate to know someone like you. . . .
Together we reach happiness,
Not as one individual, but as two.

◆ *Colleen Clyder*

A MEMORY AWAY

We have cried tears together
    and God, how we've laughed together
    and made some of our closest friends
We have talked of the fears inside us
    and the love beside us
    and we learned upon whom to depend
We have shared more with each other
    than ever before with another
    and we never had to pretend
Is there something in the air
    that brings us to care
    so deeply for others
    in such a short time?
In our final embraces
    and tears on our faces
    we sing our sad song
    of the end of our time
Though distance may come between us
    and we miss each other more with each passing day
Hold closely, my friend,
    to the love that we've shared
It's only a memory away

             ◆ *Michele Ownbey*

A friend is a present you give to yourself.

◆ *Robert Louis Stevenson*

LOVE

I love you,
Not only for what you are,
But for what I am
When I am with you.

I love you,
Not only for what
You have made of yourself,
But for what
You are making of me.

I love you
For the part of me
That you bring out;
I love you
For putting your hand
Into my heaped-up heart
And passing over
All the foolish, weak things
That you can't help

Dimly seeing there,
And for drawing out
Into the light
All the beautiful belongings
That no one else had looked
Quite far enough to find.

I love you because you
Are helping me to make
Of the lumber of my life
Not a tavern
But a temple;
Out of the works
Of my every day
Not a reproach
But a song.

I love you
Because you have done
More than any creed
Could have done
To make me good,
And more than any fate
Could have done
To make me happy.

You have done it
Without a touch,
Without a word,
Without a sign.
You have done it
By being yourself.
Perhaps that is what
Being a friend means,
After all.

◆ *Roy Croft*

Chance makes our parents, but choice makes our friends.

◆ *Jacques Delille*

CLASS SONG OF '91 [1891]

We are sighing, for time is flying,
We are going from those so dear;
Friends are severed, though 'round us gathered,
With a cheer to greet us here.
Hope is beck'ning, our fate we're reck'ning,
Life seems bright, all earth is light;
Stars are gleaming, beacons of meaning,
Lights of truth to human sight.

Then, fare you well, fare you well,
Life for us has just begun;
Don't regret, ne'er forget
This dear class of ninety-one.
Hours of pleasure, our mem'ries treasure,
Life's best moments for these we sigh;
Thoughts of gladness will scatter sadness,
When we're dreaming of days gone by.
We are sighing, for time is flying,
Soon we part from friends so dear;
Guiding teachers, God's favor'd creatures,
Ah! good-bye to all friends here.

◆ Eloise A. Bibb

MIZPAH

Go thou thy way and I go mine,
    Apart, yet not afar;
Only a thin veil hangs between
    The Pathways where we are;
And "God keep watch 'tween thee and me,"
    This is my prayer;
He looks thy way. He looketh mine,
    And keeps us near.

I know not where thy road may lie,
    Or which way mine may be;
If mine will lead through parching sands,
    And thine beside the sea;
Yet "God keeps watch 'tween thee and me."
    So never fear;
He holds thy hand, He claspeth mine,
    And keeps us near.

Should wealth and fame perchance be thine,
    And my lot lowly be,
Or you be sad or sorrowful,
    And glory be for me;
Yet "God keeps watch 'tween thee and me,"
    Both be His care,
One arm 'round thee and one 'round me
    Will keep us near.

I'll sigh sometimes to see thy face,
    But since this cannot be
I'll leave thee to the care of Him
    Who cares for thee and me.
"I'll keep thee both beneath my wings,"
    This comfort dear,
One wing o'er thee and one o'er me,
    So we are near.

And though our paths be separate
    And thy way is not mine,
Yet, coming to the mercy seat,
    My soul will meet with thine;
And "God keep watch 'tween thee and me,"
    I'll whisper there.
He blesseth thee, He blesseth me,
    And we are near.

          Julia A. Baker

You're more than a friend,
for our friendship is not questioned.
It will continue to grow
long after we have parted,
and at times
we will be close
through a passing memory
or a wondering dream.
I wish you happiness
today and tomorrow
and all the rest of the days
of your life.

          Anonymous

HOW CAN I EXPLAIN?

how can I explain
the days and ways
in which she slowly wove herself
into the lining of my life?
her eyes told tales
deeper than those we read in English
my heart responded
to those silent soliloquies
and was lost
against a background of dingy gray lockers
and crowded hallways
I fell so intensely
that at times I had to close my eyes
and hide my heart on safer ground
seeking shelter from the strength
of my own feelings
I watched her for two years
terrified to tell her how I felt
but the secret burned and had to come out
I no longer was afraid I'd die if she said no
but I was afraid I wouldn't live if I didn't try

and how can I explain
the magic of the moment

when she said yes
and became mine
how completely she consumed me
so quickly becoming
my every thought
my every dream
and my every desire
from that moment on
it was her love that was life to me
and her arms that were my home
she so encompassed me that
I could not remember a time
she had not been with me
nor conceive of a future
without her by my side

how can I explain
with only words and rhymes
the feeling of being born again my senior year
with her by my side
breathing life into me
expanding my heart
with her nearness
when I failed a test
the very sight of her would lift my spirits
when I was sore from football practice

the slightest touch from her
would heal my body
and warm me through and through
she was my best friend
my girlfriend
my biggest fan
and yes, she was my life

and how can I make you understand
the pain that came with the end
we knew it was coming
from our first hello
the only thing inevitable about our love
was the last good-bye
different religions, different colleges, different states
parents who didn't understand
wouldn't support
and eventually stopped listening
through the spring we milked the days
of every last drop of delight
and when June came
we realized our thirst for each other
was unquenchable

how can I describe the feelings on graduation day
our classmates, so happy, so carefree
and we, we lied and said we were happy
but inside, we were crying
my heart so torn I felt like I was dying
the speaker said commencement meant a new beginning
but all we could see was the end
the end of the yellow brick road
the end of the rainbow
the end of the innocence

how can I explain?

◆ *Christopher Lee*

PARENTS

This is a difficult period in our lives as we start to cross the thin line between adolescence and adulthood. We often think our parents don't understand. We need to remember that they were teenagers once, and they survived. They are willing to lend their experiences to help us survive.

◆ *Malcolm-Jamal Warner*

DEAR KAYCIE,

Good luck on your newest adventure. Eighteen years have passed very quickly—lots of good times, some tough times, but all part of becoming an adult. You have blossomed into a very responsible young adult, and your mother and I (and sisters) are very proud of you.

We have all the faith and confidence in you that you will succeed at anything you do, from college to career to someday your own family. You will be presented with many choices in the years to come, and if I could offer any advice to you, it would be don't second guess yourself. Every time you make a decision, follow your heart, and always look forward, never back—you will know in your heart if you have made the right choice.

Oh, by the way, Mom wanted to relay some additional advice: clean the lint screen after each load, don't try to iron nylons, don't stay up all night (studying or ???), and for Pete's sake, call home once a week even if you don't need money. All the other stuff you'll figure out on your own.

Take care of yourself.
Love always,
Dad

Paul Irwin

Parents can only give good advice or put them on the right paths, but the final forming of a person's character lies in their own hands.

        Anne Frank

The main reason I wanted to be successful was to get out of the ghetto. My parents helped direct my path.

        Florence Griffith Joyner

When I was a boy of fourteen, my father was so ignorant I could hardly stand to have the old man around. But when I got to be twenty-one, I was astonished by how much the old man had learned in seven years.

        Mark Twain

Parents: persons who spend half their time worrying how a child will turn out, and the rest of the time wondering when a child will turn in.

        Ted Cook

THE GIFT

It was a warm summer day when the gods placed it in her hands. She trembled with emotion as she saw how fragile it appeared. This was a very special gift the gods were entrusting to her. A gift that would one day belong to the world. Until then, they instructed her, she was to be its guardian and protector. The woman said she understood and reverently took it home, determine to live up to the faith the gods had placed in her.

At first she barely let it out of her sight, protecting it from anything she perceived to be harmful to its well-being; watching with fear in her heart when it was exposed to the environment outside of the sheltered cocoon she had formed around it. But the woman began to realize that she could not shelter it forever. It needed to learn to survive the harsh elements in order to grow strong. So with gentle care she gave it more space to grow, enough to allow it to grow wild and untamed.

Sometimes she would lie in bed at night, feelings of inadequacy overwhelming her. She wondered if she was capable of handling the awesome responsibility placed on her. Then she would hear the quiet whispers of the gods reassuring her that they knew she was doing her best. And she would fall asleep feeling comforted.

The woman grew more at ease with her responsibility as the years passed. The gift had enriched her life in so many ways by its very presence that she could no longer remember what her life had been like before receiving it. She had all but forgotten her agreement with the gods.

One day she became aware of how much the gift had changed. It no longer had a look of vulnerability about it. Now it seemed to glow with strength and steadiness, almost as if it were developing a power within. Month after month she watched as it became stronger and more powerful, and the woman remembered her promise. She knew deep within her heart that her time with the gift was nearing an end.

The inevitable day arrived when the gods came to take the gift and present it to the world. The woman felt a deep sadness, for she would miss its constant presence in her life. With heartfelt gratitude, she thanked the gods for allowing her the privilege of watching over the precious gift for so many years. Straightening her shoulders, she stood proud, knowing it was, indeed, a very special gift. One that would add to the beauty and essence of the world around it. And the mother let her child go.

◆ *Renee R. Vroman*

Sometimes we need to fuse our lives again with those people who seem at times to be antagonists—you young men especially, because it is hard for us men to profess our love. It is quite often very difficult for your fathers and you. So for you young men, when the ceremony is over, I want you to run over to the old man. Grab him, hug him, and kiss him and say, "Dad, I love you and I thank you for all the years." That's part of the ceremony. I demand that of you when this is all over. It will save you a lot of trouble getting to know your father ten years from now.

◆ *Ray Bradbury*

GROWING

I'm leaving now to slay the foe—
Fight the battles, high and low.

I'm leaving, Mother, hear me go!
Please wish me luck today.

I've grown my wings, I want to fly,
Seize my victories where they lie.
I'm going, Mom, but please don't cry—
Just let me find my way.

I want to see and touch and hear,
Though there are dangers, there are fears.
I'll smile my smiles and dry my tears—
Please let me speak my say.

I'm off to find my world, my dreams,
Carve my niche, sew my seams,
Remember, as I sail my streams—
I'll love you, all the way.

◆ *Brooke Mueller*

You were the best thing—one of the best things—that came along
and happened to us. . . . You were an amazing event in our lives. You
were truly, truly amazing. You were a great stroke of wonderful, wonderful luck. . . .

Parents are cheerful and forward-looking people. We are inherently hopeful. And we looked forward to the time when you walked,

and to your first words, and to your first sentences. Some of you, we're still looking forward to your first good paragraphs, but we're hopeful.

We are inherently looking out for the best. We are terribly proud of you . . . and to see you here, in some ways relieved that you didn't have to live our lives all over again. It's a sobering thing to bring a child into this world, an act of vanity at the beginning, to produce somebody who is just exactly like yourself—too much so. And then the pride that we have in you now, to see you as you take steps toward independence, and to walk through that door, which you have to do, so you can forgive us, and then you can walk back in sometime, and something else will happen. We can be friends of some sort. . . .

And most of all, we are proud of having produced you. We have high hopes for you—high hopes. And speaking in behalf of your parents, I want to tell you how much we love all of you.

God bless you—God bless you as much as God blessed us when he sent you along.

Garrison Keillor

I have loved
watching you go through life
as only a child can . . .
    laughing, crying,
      so sure of yourself,
and at the same time
      so often full of doubts.

My heart broke for you
    when life was unfair;
I would have shielded you
from pain and heartache
    if you had let me.

I wanted to protect you,
but you needed to grow
into your own person,
so I had to let go of you—
a little at a time.
That was one of the hardest
things I've ever had to do.

Your childhood is gone now,
    and I still miss those
    wonderful times,
but I am so proud of
the adult you have become.
I love you,
and whatever paths in life
you may choose to embrace,
    my love will be with you. . .
and I will cherish you always.

◆ *Peggy Selig*

HER LITTLE BOY

Always a "little boy" to her,
    No matter how old he's grown,
Her eyes are blind to the strands of gray,
    She's deaf to his manly tone.
His voice is the same as the day he asked,
"What makes the old cat purr?"
Ever and ever he's just the same—
    A little boy to her.

Always a "little boy" to her,
    She heeds not the lines of care
That furrow his face—to her it is still
    As it was in his boyhood, fair;
His hopes and his joys are as dear to her
    As they were in his small-boy days.
He never changes; to her he's still
"My little boy," she says.

Always a "little boy" to her,
    And to him she's the mother fair,
With the laughing eyes and the cheering smile
    Of the boyhood days back there.
Back there, somewhere in the midst of years—
    Back there with the childish joy,

Never let your parents chaperone
a school dance.

And to her he is never the man we see,
  But always, "her little boy."

Always a "little boy" to her,
  The ceaseless march of the years
Goes rapidly by, but its drumbeats die
  Ere ever they reach her ears.
The smile that she sees is the smile of youth,
  The wrinkles are dimples of joy,
His hair with its gray is as sunny as May,
  He is always "her little boy."

◆ *Pearson's Weekly*

NEW BEGINNINGS

Dear Graduate,

Well, this is it! Graduation is over and you're ready to begin life's journey! I know you have lots of mixed feelings. That's the weird thing about most of life's big moments—very rarely do they consist of one emotion. But that's okay. It helps to make the good times more precious and the not-so-good times bearable.

I've spent a lot of time trying to figure out what sage advice I could pass along. That's one of the hard parts about being a parent—determining what should be said and what should be left for you to discover. I finally decided just to offer a little insight to life's basic questions. Some people go through their whole lives without ever giving them any thought. Too bad—as you search for the answers, you can make some wonderful discoveries. They can also be frustrating; just when you think you've found the answer, you'll find the need to ask another question. (Which explains why even at my incredibly advanced age, I still don't have any answers!) At any rate, I hope that sharing this little piece of myself and my soul will somehow help to carry you through when the questions come along.

Who? It took me a while to realize that this is probably the most important question of all. Take time to discover who you are and be your own person. Strive to be honest, respectful, and happy. When you are at peace with yourself, everything else will fall into place. Just be careful not to wrap your identity in possessions. Allow yourself to grow and change. And remember always that you are not alone—you have your family, your friends, your guardian angel, and God (not necessarily in that order!).

What? This is a tricky one, and at first this question had me fooled. I thought the question was, "What will I do today?" However, I found that things really got interesting when I instead asked, *"What is my passion?"* Discover what it is that burns inside and keeps you going, then nurture it. Take it apart and build it back together. Do whatever you want with it, but never let it from your sight. Do it because that's what you love to do. The joy it brings you will keep you going through some of the doldrums of life.

When? This is a sneaky one. Do not ignore it. It will keep you balanced. Some things are best done now. Procrastination usually just creates more work. But keep in mind that there is a season for everything, and some things are better left for another day. As hard as it may be, remember to take time to rest and enjoy the miracle of each new day. With practice, you will learn the pleasure of doing some things now and the unique delight of waiting and planning for others.

Where? Surprisingly, this is the easiest one. You will always have the answer with you if you keep your home in your heart and put your heart into wherever you call home. Be an active part of your community and you will discover the special charm that will endear it to you. Remember always that the simplest act of kindness can make an enormous difference, and that you can change the world.

Why? Never stop asking this one. It's the one that will keep you growing. Let it. Let it challenge you when you've become too complacent. Let it shout at you when you are making important decisions. Let it whisper to you when you've lost sight of who you are or where you want to be. But you also need to be careful with this one. Sometimes the answer does not come for years, and sometimes it doesn't come at all. Recognizing that basic fact can keep you sane and allow you to move on.

How? Ah, this is the one on which I can't advise you! This is the one you will answer in your own special way. But you've come so far in the past few years, I know that you'll do fine. Just remember to believe in yourself and in miracles. Remember that the greatest discovering comes after stumbling over questions. And please remember—always—that I love you.

Congratulations on your new beginning.

Love,

Mom

◆ *Paula (Bachleda) Koskey*

"Oh, look at this! Our little girl coming home from her first date! You kids just go ahead and say good night as though we're not even here!"

LOUISE COYLE

My mother, living in the past tense,
Has kept every school report I've ever written,
Also every tooth I've lost, every award I've won.
At least once a week, she
Takes out the family photo albums
And conducts a walking tour across the
Cellophaned pages, across the years.
She has frozen me in time,
A still-life picture
In the gold-locket chamber of her heart.

Mama, I want to get out of high school,
Get out of the house,
Get out of the past.
I don't want to be ten years old forever.
I want to have my own apartment
And when I do, I'll call you regularly, I promise.
I'll even come over for dinner,
At least once a week.
And we'll look at the old pictures together.

         ◆ *Mel Glenn*

The Meaning of Success

◆ ◆ ◆

All you need in this life is ignorance and confidence, and then success is sure.

Mark Twain

The American Dream means giving it your all, trying your hardest, accomplishing something. And then I'd add to that, giving something back. No definition of a successful life can do anything but include serving others.

George Bush

Eighty percent of success is showing up.

Woody Allen

We are prone to judge success by the index of our salaries or the size of our automobiles rather than by the quality of our service and relationship to mankind.

Martin Luther King, Jr.

The world has a way of giving what is demanded of it. If you are frightened and look for failure and poverty, you will get them, no matter how hard you may try to succeed. Lack of faith in yourself, in what life will do for you, cuts you off from the good things of the world. Expect victory and you make victory.

Pristine Bradley

You want to know the biggest illusion about success? That it's like a pinnacle to be climbed, a thing to be possessed, or a static result to be achieved. If you want to succeed, if you want to achieve all your outcomes, you have to think of success as a process, a way of life, a habit of mind, a strategy for life.

Anthony Robbins

I still say I'm a little different, because success to me is not having the most money, or having the biggest car or the biggest house. Success is just being happy.

Herschel Walker

Success is a journey not a destination. The doing is usually more important than the outcome. Not everyone can be Number 1.

Arthur Ashe

Success is counted sweetest
By those who ne'er succeed.

Emily Dickinson

I had a vision I could succeed. You have to believe that you can succeed, believe that you can be whatever your heart desires, and be willing to work for it.

◆ *Oprah Winfrey*

Success is like a fart — only your own smells nice.

◆ *James P. Hogan*

On life's report card, attitude counts, enthusiasm counts, a commitment to lifelong learning counts, hard work counts, and helping others counts. If you go all-out, you will feel the difference in the quality of your life, and that is what success is all about.

◆ *Steve Lodle*

Success is doing what you want to do, when you want, where you want, with whom you want, as much as you want.

◆ *Anthony Robbins*

I'd rather be a failure at something I love than a success at something I hate.

◆ *George Burns*

Let no feeling of discouragement prey upon you, and in the end you are sure to succeed.

◆ *Abraham Lincoln*

The first principle of success is desire — knowing what you want. Desire is the planting of your seed.

Robert Collier

Enthusiasm is a vital element toward the individual success of every man or woman.

Conrad Hilton

A man cannot be said to succeed in life who does not satisfy one friend.

Henry David Thoreau

The only thing that separates successful people from the ones who aren't is the willingness to work very, very hard.

Helen Gurley Brown

We act as though comfort and luxury were the chief requirements of life, when all that we need to make us happy is something to be enthusiastic about.

Charles Kingsley

I owe my success to having listened respectfully to the very best advice, and then going away and doing the exact opposite.

G. K. Chesterton

I claim to be no more than an average man with below average capabilities. I have not the shadow of a doubt that any man or woman can achieve what I have if he or she would put forth the same effort and cultivate the same hope and faith.

◆ *Mahatma Gandhi*

Success rests with the courage, endurance, and, above all, the will to become the person you are, however peculiar that may be. . . . Then you will be able to say, "I have found my hero and he is me."

◆ *George Sheehan*

Flaming enthusiasm, backed up by horse sense and persistence, is the quality that most frequently makes for success.

◆ *Dale Carnegie*

Sometimes I worry about being a success in a mediocre world.

◆ *Lily Tomlin*

To burn always with this hard gem-like flame, to maintain this ecstasy, is success in life.

◆ *Walter Pater*

Success is peace of mind in knowing you did your best.

◆ *John Wooden*

The real secret of success is enthusiasm. Yes, more than enthusiasm, I would say excitement. I like to see men get excited. When they get excited they make a success of their lives.

◆ *Walter Chrysler*

Any fact facing us is not as important as our attitude toward it, for that determines our success or failure.

◆ *Norman Vincent Peale*

Once you get rid of the idea that you must please other people before you please yourself, and you begin to follow your own instincts—only then can you be successful. You become more satisfied, and when you are other people tend to be satisfied by what you do.

◆ *Raquel Welch*

What is success? I think it is a mixture of having a flair for the thing that you are doing; knowing that it is not enough, that you have got to have hard work and a certain sense of purpose.

◆ *Margaret Thatcher*

The victory of success is half won when one gains the habit of setting goals and achieving them. Even the most tedious chore will become endurable as you parade through each day convinced that every task, no matter how menial or boring, brings you closer to fulfilling your dreams.

◆ *Og Mandino*

It's very difficult for me to even see myself as successful because I still see myself as in the process of becoming successful. To me, "successful" is getting to the point where you are absolutely comfortable with yourself. And it does not matter how many things you have acquired.

◆   *Oprah Winfrey*

Instead of thinking about where you are, think about where you want to be. It takes twenty years of hard work to become an overnight success.

◆   *Diana Rankin*

The difference between a successful person and others is not a lack of strength, not a lack of knowledge, but rather in a lack of will.

◆   *Vince Lombardi*

True success is overcoming the fear of being unsuccessful.

◆   *Paul Sweeney*

Success is the child of audacity.

◆   *Benjamin Disraeli*

Patience, persistence and perspiration make an unbeatable combination for success.

◆   *Napoleon Hill*

The successful man will profit from his mistakes and try again in a different way.

◆   *Dale Carnegie*

Perseverance is a great element of success. If you only knock long enough and loud enough at the gate, you are sure to wake somebody up.

Henry Wadsworth Longfellow

Always bear in mind that your own resolution to succeed is more important than any other one thing.

Abraham Lincoln

That man is a success who has lived well, laughed often and loved much.

Robert Louis Stevenson

Many of us are afraid to follow our passions, to pursue what we want most because it means taking risks and even facing failure. But to pursue your passion with all your heart and soul is success in itself. The greatest failure is to have never really tried.

Robyn Allan

I have learned that success is to be measured not so much by the position that one has reached in life as by the obstacles which he has overcome while trying to succeed.

Booker T. Washington

There is only one success . . . to be able to spend your life your own way, and not to give others absurd maddening claims upon it.

Christopher Morley

We must walk consciously only part way toward our goal, and then leap in the dark to our success.

Henry David Thoreau

Try to think of success as a journey, an adventure, not a specific destination. Your goals may change during the course of that journey, and your original ambitions may be superseded by different, larger ones.

Michael Korda

All of us attain the greatest success and happiness possible in this life whenever we use our native capacities to their fullest extent. . . . And every life must be chalked up at least a partial failure when it does not succeed in reaching its inherent destiny.

Smiley Blanton

You always pass failure on the way to success.

Mickey Rooney

All the money in the world doesn't mean a thing if you don't have time to enjoy it.

Oprah Winfrey

Sometimes success is due less to ability than zeal. The winner is he who gives himself to his work body and soul.

Charles Buxton

The grand essentials to happiness in this life are something to do, something to love and something to hope for.

❖ *Joseph Addison*

What's money? A man is a success if he gets up in the morning and goes to bed at night and in between does what he wants to do.

❖ *Bob Dylan*

Success is not the result of spontaneous combustion. You must set yourself on fire.

❖ *Reggie Leach*

Success is not built on what we accomplish for ourselves. Its foundation lies in what we do for others.

❖ *Danny Thomas*

The only true happiness comes from squandering ourselves for a purpose.

❖ *William Cowper*

All I would tell people is to hold on to what was individual about themselves, not to allow their ambition for success to cause them to try to imitate the success of others. You've got to find it on your own terms.

❖ *Harrison Ford*

Most people think of it in terms of getting; success, however, begins in terms of giving.

Henry Ford

If you have a good name, if you are right more often than you are wrong, if your children respect you, if your grandchildren are glad to see you, if your friends can count on you and you can count on them in time of trouble, if you can face your God and say "I have done my best," then you are a success.

Ann Landers

The secret of success is constancy to purpose.

Benjamin Franklin

Self-trust is the first secret of success.

Ralph Waldo Emerson

How few people realize that success in life depends more upon what they are than upon what they know.

Charles Wesley

Don't be afraid of trying, of dreaming. Don't even be afraid of failure, or tears. We all stumble, we all face fear—that's of course what makes us human. But none of us should ever regret. None of us should ever sit at a grandchild's graduation and think, "I wish that were me starting out all over again. There's so much I would do differently."

You have a lifetime of chances in your grasp right now. Don't lose any of them. And don't give up the chance to take a risk or follow a vision, to touch a life or hug a child. Touching a life—that's what I want to talk to you briefly about today. Each of you has visions of success for your future, and your own ways to define it. And let me give you mine.

I believe, and I said this when I was president, that any definition of a successful life in America must include service to others. And it's just that simple.

And it doesn't mean that you have to run for public office, though I hope some of you will be actively involved in one way or another in our political system.

But serving others does mean rolling up your sleeves and getting involved in your community. And it means getting off the sidelines, and it means being a doer and not a critic. And it means contributing to a cause larger than yourself. It's what I call being one of a thousand Points of Light.

And there is no problem we face as a nation—you've got to think about this—there's not one single problem facing this country that is not being solved in some level, someplace in our country. And for eight years as vice-president and four as president, and today too, I have seen literally thousands of examples of the neighbor-helping-neighbor spirit that made this country the kindest and the strongest in the world. And that was one of the real joys of being president, and Barbara and I are continuing to try to encourage others to volunteer their time and effort to solving community problems.

People said, Was it difficult going from the White House back to your little house in Houston, Texas? Wasn't difficult at all. We fit right in, doing what we did fifty years ago, when we were first married. I believe, you see, that we really do need a kinder and gentler nation.

Government has an obligation to help, and yet there is something special, very special about the kindness of a neighbor helping someone he or she might not even know.

No exercise is better for the human heart than reaching down and lifting someone else up. To serve others, to enrich your community—this truly defines a successful life. And success is personal, and it is charitable. It is the sum not of our possessions, but of how we help others. . . .

So be bold in your dreaming; be bold in your living; be bold in your caring, your compassion, your humanity. And put aside cynicism and count your blessings and do something to help others. Then when you sit at your grandchild's commencement half a century from now, you'll look back at the tapestry of your life and find it good. And that, my fellow classmates, will be your greatest success of all.

◆ *George Bush*

If you want to be great, you must serve willingly and love greatly.

◆ *Cornel West*

Difficulties call out great qualities and make success possible. Remember, it's a stiff wind that allows the eagle to soar higher.

◆ *Vanessa Williams*

The important thing is not how much money a person makes, it is what he does with it that matters.

◆ *Arthur P. Gaston*

I never thought of achievement. I just did what came along for me to do—the thing that gave me the most pleasure.

◆ *Eleanor Roosevelt*

Good people are good because they've come to wisdom through failure. We get very little wisdom from success, you know.

◆ *William Saroyan*

Failure is, in a sense, the highway to success, inasmuch as every discovery of what is false leads us to seek earnestly after what is true, and every fresh experience points out some form of error which we shall afterward carefully avoid.

◆ *William Kits*

Success can also cause misery. The trick is not to be surprised when you discover it doesn't bring you all the happiness and answers you thought it would.

◆ *The Artist Formerly Known As Prince*

I know the price of success: dedication, hard work and an unremitting devotion to the things you want to see happen.

◆ *Frank Lloyd Wright*

There are no secrets to success. It is the result of preparation, hard work, learning from failure.

Gen. Colin L. Powell

The most important single ingredient in the formula of success is knowing how to get along with people.

Theodore Roosevelt

Success (as opposed to $ucce$$) is making your living at what you would do even if you weren't paid to do it.

Artie Shaw

Success is not so much what we have as it is what we are.

Troy Aikman

Success is doing what you love to do, with people that you love, in an environment that you love.

Wally Amos

Success is having real love in your life. Everything else is just killing time.

Kenny Loggins

The dictionary is the only place where success comes before work.

Arthur Brisbane

One of the first things that a young person must internalize, deep down in the blood and bones, is the understanding that although he may encounter many defeats, he must not be defeated. If life teaches us anything, it may be that it's necessary to suffer some defeats. Look at a diamond: It is the result of extreme pressure. Less pressure, it is crystal; less than that, it's coal; and less than that, it is fossilized leaves or just plain dirt. It's necessary, therefore, to be tough enough to bite the bullet as it is shot into one's mouth, to bite it and stop it before it tears a hole in one's throat. One must learn to care for oneself first, so that one can then dare to care for someone else. That's what it takes to make the caged bird sing.

◆ *Maya Angelou*

I studied the lives of great men and famous women, and I found that the men and women who got to the top were those who did the jobs they had in hand, with everything they had of energy and enthusiasm and hard work.

◆ *Harry S. Truman*

If you're not happy every morning when you get up, leave for work, or start to work at home—if you're not enthusiastic about doing that, you're not going to be successful.

◆ *Donald M. Kendall*

Put your heart, mind, intellect, and soul even to your smallest acts. This is the secret of success.

◆ *Swami Sivananda*

Success is a state of mind. If you want success, start thinking of yourself as a success.

◆ *Joyce Brothers*

Would you like me to give you a formula for . . . success? It's quite simple, really. Double your rate of failure . . . You're thinking of failure as the enemy of success. But it isn't at all. . . . You can be discouraged by failure—or you can learn from it. So go ahead and make mistakes. Make all you can. Because, remember, that's where you'll find success. On the far side of failure.

◆ *Thomas J. Watson*

Success is the ability to close the door on your past, regardless of your failures, and move forward. In other words, if you're not on the way, you're in the way, so it's best that you get out of the way.

◆ *Bill White*

If you find it in your heart to care for somebody else, you will have succeeded.

◆ *Maya Angelou*

I cannot give you the formula for success, but I can give you the formula for failure—try to please everybody.

◆ *Herbert Bayard Swope*

I believe the difference between an eminently successful person and one whose life is just mediocre is the difference between a person who had an aim, a focus, a model upon which he superimposed his own life and one who didn't. To put it bluntly, you can't get anywhere unless you know where to start from and where to go.

◆ *Lionel Barrymore*

Success seems to be largely a matter of hanging on after others have let go.

◆ *William Feather*

GOAL

More than a destination,
It's the journey to your goal.
Success is a process,
And planning plays a role.

You must know where you're going
To know when you are there.
Your planning must be proper
Or you'll end up who knows where.

Life will be its happiest
While you pursue your goal.
A goal gives you confidence—
It turns the meek to bold.

Commit your goal to paper,
And read it every day.
Headed in the right direction,
You're sure to find your way.

You then will not be living
In disharmony and strife.
You will know where you are going—
You have just designed your life.

◆ *Don B. Decker*

Success doesn't come to you. You go to it.

◆ *Marva Collins*

Failure is success if we learn from it.

◆ *Malcolm Forbes*

To feel true success find an inner joy of self.
Life is full of material illusions which cannot buy success.
True success comes from within.

◆ *Tova Borgnine*

To laugh often and much, to win the respect of intelligent people and the affection of children; to earn the appreciation of honest critics and endure the betrayal of false friends; to appreciate beauty; to find the best in others; to leave the world a bit better, whether by a healthy child, a garden patch or a redeemed social condition; to know even one life has breathed easier because you have lived. This is to have succeeded.

◆ *Ralph Waldo Emerson*

A man can succeed at almost anything for which he has unlimited enthusiasm.

◆ *Charles M. Schwab*

Do your job naturally because you like it and success will take care of itself.

◆ *Norman Vincent Peale*

If *A* is success in life, then *A* equals *X* plus *Y* plus *Z*. Work is *X*, *Y* is play, and *Z* is keeping your mouth shut.

◆ *Albert Einstein*

Some people see their degree as a ticket to success. In my view and my experience, it's not a ticket that guarantees you'll go someplace. It is a passport—an invaluable passport that opens the door to wherever you might choose to travel, so long as your passport is renewed regularly.

For in your journey, be assured that along with success you'll face obstacles, disappointments, maybe some inequities, surprises and, most of all . . . most of all . . . continual change. So please don't assume that your learning stops today. To the contrary, the real value of your degree comes not only from what you have learned but from your willingness and ability to continue learning throughout your life. And to me, knowing that there's so much left to discover, so much left to experience, makes life an exciting adventure . . . an exhilarating ride that's always interesting.

A commencement means a beginning, not an ending. May this commencement, this beginning, launch you on an exciting and fulfilling journey of achievement and personal happiness.

◆ *James S. Hunt*

'Tis a lesson you should heed,
Try, try again.
If at first you don't succeed,
Try, try again.

◆ *W. E. Hickson*

My mother drew a distinction between achievement and success. She said that achievement is the knowledge that you have studied and worked hard and done the best that is in you. Success is being praised by others, and that's nice, too, but not as important or satisfying. Always aim for achievement and forget about success.

◆ *Helen Hayes*

Individuals who succeed have a belief in the power of commitment. If there's a single belief that seems almost inseparable from success, it's that there's no great success without great commitment. If you look at successful people in any field, you'll find they're not necessarily the best and the brightest, the fastest and the strongest. You'll find they're the ones with the most commitment. The great Russian ballerina Anna Pavlova once said, "To follow, without halt, one aim: there's the secret of success."

Anthony Robbins

Success, to me, is embodied by the last great New York Yankees outfielder, Mickey Mantle. Mickey Mantle hit 536 home runs in his lifetime. Indeed he is remembered as a home-run hitter. But he also struck out 1,710 times.

Every time Mantle went to the plate, he had the same chance to do either. Yet, he kept going to the plate and swinging for those fences. As his record indicates, sometimes he connected; more often he didn't.

But as Robert Kennedy once said, "Only those who dare to fail miserably can achieve greatly."

Success means daring to fail—a lesson we all can learn.

Rieva Lesonsky

Success is usually measured in terms of what we're remembered for. Keeping this in mind, I thought my kids would remember me as a woman who wrote twelve books, received sixteen honorary doctorates, and wrote for 31 million newspaper readers a week. My daughter told me that she would always remember me for caving in and buying her a stupid leather coat she thought she'd die if she didn't have . . . and ended up wearing once.

So you see, success isn't necessarily a monument to achievement, but small acts of love.

◆ *Erma Bombeck*

I have learned that no matter how successful or proficient or accomplished I might think I am, I am always going to make mistakes. I will always have to face some difficulties. I am always going to have to deal with the possibility of failure, and I will always be able to utilize these things in my work. So I am no longer afraid of becoming lost, because the journey back always reveals to me something new about my life and my own humanity.

◆ *Billy Joel*

Many of the most successful men I have known have never grown up. They have retained bubbling-over boyishness. They have relished wit, they have indulged in humor. They have not allowed "dignity" to depress them into moroseness. Youthfulness of spirit is the twin brother of optimism, and optimism is the stuff of which American business success is fashioned. Resist growing up.

◆ *B. C. Forbes*

I am famous. That is a large part of why I was asked to speak here today. . . . It is a large part of the reason I received an honorary doctorate today when in fact I don't even have a bachelor's degree—because I'm famous. I would like to think that it's also because I'm a pretty good guy and I'm passionate about my craft and my business, but it's not. It's because I'm famous and the funny thing is that my fame is a complete accident. . . . Fame, this thing that I have, is very rare, very strange, and very meaningless. It is a poor measure of success. . . . Look beyond the veneer of what you consider success. I would like you to try to focus now and for the rest of your lives not on glory but greatness.

◆ *Jason Alexander*

DON'T QUIT

When things go wrong as they sometimes will,
When the road you're trudging seems all uphill,
When the funds are low, and the debts are high,
And you want to smile, but you have to sigh,
When care is pressing you down a bit—
Rest if you must, but don't you quit.

Success is failure turned inside out,
The silver tint of the clouds of doubt,
And you never can tell how close you are,
It may be near when it seems afar,
So, stick to the fight when you're hardest hit—
It's when things go wrong that you mustn't quit.

◆ *Author unknown*

I believe that a successful life is one that springs from the deep intuition of the heart—finding a passion, a calling that not only fulfills our dreams, but leads us to be of service to family, friend, and community. Once that calling is clear, true success lies in living with kindness and respect as constant companions in all one's undertakings.

◆ *Gloria Loring*

What matters is how you choose to love. As you know, there's a lot of emphasis placed on success, and I hear it all the time. But what I know is there is no success where there is no joy, so instead of looking for success in your life, look for the thing that is going to bring you the greatest joy. Joy is the only goal really worth seeking.

◆ *Oprah Winfrey*

If you want to achieve success, all you really need to do is find a way to model those who have already succeeded. That is, find out what actions they took, specifically how they used their brain and body to produce the results you desire to duplicate. If you want to be a better friend, a richer person, a better parent, a better athlete, a more successful businessman, all you need to do is find models of excellence.

◆ *Anthony Robbins*

People with passion find it difficult to use the word *work*. Such people are pursuing what they most enjoy and what is personally rewarding. Everyone is born with a limited amount of time. Every moment we live—whether we're working, playing, complaining, or being thankful—is time that we've spent. Nothing is more valuable than the time we have left. When we're pursuing our passion, it isn't just getting to the goal, because the journey is as rewarding as the end result. At the end of our lives we can say, "I've loved my life"—the ultimate definition of success.

◆ *Cynthia Kersey*

ABRAHAM LINCOLN

Failed in business at age 21.
Was defeated in a legislative race at 22.
Failed again in business at age 24.
Overcame the death of his sweetheart at age 26.
Had a nervous breakdown at age 27.
Lost a congressional race at age 34.
Lost a congressional race at age 36.
Lost a senatorial race at age 45.
Failed in an effort to become vice-president at age 47.
Lost a senatorial race at age 49.
Was elected president of the United States at age 52.

Success means we go to sleep at night knowing that our talents and abilities were used in a way that served others. We're compensated by grateful looks in people's eyes, whatever material abundance supports us in performing joyfully and at high energy, and the magnificent feeling that we did our bit today to save the world.

◆ *Marianne Williamson*

Make sure that the career you choose is one you enjoy. If you don't enjoy what you're doing, it will be difficult to give the extra time, effort, and devotion it takes to be a success. If it is a career that you find fun and enjoyable, then you will do whatever it takes. You will give freely of your time and effort and you will not feel that you are making a sacrifice in order to be a success.

◆ *Kathy Whitworth*

The traditional version tells us that there are two things you need to succeed: talent and hunger, or drive. I have added a third thing, and that is optimism. You can have all the talent in the world, but if you don't believe you can overcome failure, if you do not mentally rehearse success, then your talent and drive will come to nothing once you have been knocked down.

◆ *Martin Seligman*

I think the thing, the one thing that has allowed me to certainly achieve both material success and spiritual success, is the ability to listen to my instinct. I call it my inner voice. It doesn't matter what you call it — nature, instinct, higher power. It's the ability to understand the difference between what your heart is saying and what your head is saying. I now always go with the heart.

◆ *Oprah Winfrey*

I love to talk to kids and ask them where they're going to college, and what they want to study. And so often it's all planned. They know exactly where they're going, what they're going to do and where they're going to be ten years from now. I don't want to dampen their enthusiasm, but I want to say, "You can't plan everything." I never planned to write books, it was not something I ever thought about. I thought I'd be a lawyer for the rest of my life. It's important to have goals and to work hard for them, but life has a way of presenting opportunities that you don't really notice at first. Success a lot of times depends on whether you make a change and try something that you hadn't planned, something new.

◆ *John Grisham*

Ask yourself the secret of your success. Listen to your answer, and practice it.

◆ *Richard Bach*

Life's Meaning

◆ ◆ ◆

The sole meaning of life is to serve humanity.

Leo Tolstoy

You don't get to choose how you're going to die. Or when. You can only decide how you're going to live. Now.

Joan Baez

Do not fear death so much, but rather the inadequate life.

Bertolt Brecht

In the end, nothing we do or say in this lifetime will matter as much as the way we have loved each other.

Daphne Rose Kingma

In the long run we shape our lives and we shape ourselves. The process never ends until we die. And the choices we make are ultimately our own responsibility.

Eleanor Roosevelt

Only a life lived for others is a life worth while.

◆ *Albert Einstein*

My philosophy is that not only are you responsible for your life, but doing the best at this moment puts you in the best place for the next moment.

◆ *Oprah Winfrey*

Life is short. Live it up.

◆ *Nikita Khrushchev*

Until you know that life is interesting, and find it so, you haven't found your soul.

◆ *Geoffrey Fisher*

Some of the most important things in life aren't things.

◆ *Linda Ellerbee*

There are only two ways to live your life. One is as though nothing is a miracle. The other is as though everything is a miracle.

◆ *Albert Einstein*

To be alive, to be able to see, to walk, to have houses, music, paintings—it's all a miracle. I have adopted the technique of living life from miracle to miracle.

◆ *Arthur Rubinstein*

Three things in human life are important: the first is to be kind. The second is to be kind. The third is to be kind.

◆ *Henry James*

Life is what we are alive to. It is not length but breadth. To be alive only to appetite, pleasure, pride, money-making, and not to goodness, kindness, purity, love, history, poetry, music, flowers, stars, God, and eternal hope is to be all but dead.

◆ *Mattbie D. Babcock*

The only thing worth living for is the lifting up of our fellow men.

◆ *Booker T. Washington*

Life is about enjoying yourself and having a good time.

◆ *Cher*

The purpose of life, after all, is to live it, to taste experience to the utmost, to reach out eagerly and without fear for newer and richer experience.

◆ *Eleanor Roosevelt*

Life is short. Be swift to love! Make haste to be kind.

◆ *Henri F. Amiel*

I have found that if you love life, life will love you back.

◆ *Arthur Rubinstein*

LIFE IS ALL TOO SHORT:
WAYS TO MAKE IT THE BEST IT CAN BE

As witnessed by the tragic death of Princess Diana, life can be much too short no matter what our station in life, our good health, or our benevolent nature.

The following are actions to take, things to contemplate, and simple philosophies that can help all of us have a life that is as full and positive as possible regardless of how long we are here in this lifetime.

1. Give and Experience As Much Love As Possible: Love is probably the best gift we can give to ourselves first, then to others in our lifetime. It behooves us all to learn to fully love ourselves first, and then pass that love on to our family, friends, and, in a more "humanitarian" way, to all those with whom we come into contact. It is not often easy for us to give unconditional love to others, in part due to the way we learned about love from our parents and society growing up. To change that, and give at least the "brotherly" form of love to all we meet and know, is to practice true acceptance, and it will come back to us often.

2. Forgive and Let Go of All You Feel Has Wronged You: Let it go. Make a list of all the people from childhood to the present you feel hurt or wronged you in some way. It is sometimes

helpful to ask yourself if "you" had any responsibility in the way things occurred. Then let it go. Write them a letter stating you forgive them (which can be mailed or thrown away after writing). Get yourself "complete" with the past. Just one negative grudge or ill feeling held on to can make it very hard for you to have any truly positive and successful relationships now or in the future.

3. Do What You Are Good At and Love to Do: If you are sitting behind a desk from eight to five every day working for someone else, and you dislike your job or your working environment, take steps to change it! Write out what you are good at and what you really love in your heart to do. Then go after it! If it means changing jobs, locations, or working for yourself, do it. Being true to yourself and your God-given talents and desires will make your life so much happier in the end it will be worth it. When you can say you love your work and those you work with, you will have a much more stress-free life, and the legacy you leave behind will be great and cherished by the people you touched with your genuine actions and words.

4. Be *Positive* in All That You Think, Say, and Do: Get rid of any *guilt* feelings you have, develop and trust your *intuition*, learn to quit *worrying*, visualize and affirm being *successful* and *prosperous*, develop and *keep* great *faith*, learn to deal with

anger so it is not destructive to you or others, be totally *responsible*, learn to identify and control your *stress*, live *one day* at a time, and finally, *trust* a *higher power* or Universal Law to help you in your life journey and give you some support along the way.

The choice is ours how we live our life. Many believe the true foundation of all that is great and lasting in the world is based on love. Love is a core value. And it is always there as a choice for us to use in our life or not.

"Only one life that soon is past; Only what's done with love will last."

◆ *Dennis R. Tesdell*

THE DANCE

The most difficult thing to face and deal with is your life. What is it? What do you want it to be? What should it be? What do you do to achieve it? What's acceptable? What's kosher? What's not?

Is life a wild snake that has eaten peyote and is compulsively thrashing about, taking you where it wants to go, frightening you, threatening or actually biting you, coiling around your neck and strangling you, or simply poisoning you until you're dead? Are you following the mesmerizing undulations and dancing to the serpent's tune, unable to do anything as the clock ticks? Is this the way it is? No.

It's not true. The snake can be guided, led, seduced, cajoled, and instructed.

Life need not be something we are in awe of, overwhelmed and frightened by. Nor do we need to be continually critical in our approach to life. Awe, fear, and criticism of our own lives, or of others', lead us to a lower self-esteem, a disastrous response. Not a good resolution for life. These ways retard us and relegate us to second banana, supporting player, an extra in some sumptuous Hollywood extravaganza. In truth, it's your movie the whole way. You're the writer, producer, director, and lead actor, and it's all based on your original story and idea.

What you do in the course of your life—your choices—creates your story line, your journey. It's important what you do, but how you do it is what really counts. That's what it's all about. There is an art to doing whatever you do. There is an art to living. Can you choose? Can you determine? Can you make it go as you wish? Can you decide, then execute? Yes. Yes. Yes.

Life is yours. It can be understood. It can be seen. If it can be seen, it can be won. You are not in a rudderless barge on a rampaging river that just takes you endlessly downstream. It's really possible for you to look the snake square in the eye, transform its poison into a serum, its bite into a kiss, its coiled strangulation into an embrace, its mesmerizing dance into your tango. It's yours. You are the snake. You are the dancer and the dance.

◆ *Milton Katselas*

Life is truly a ride. We're all strapped in and no one can stop it. When the doctor slaps your behind, he's ripping your ticket and away you go. As you make each passage from youth to adulthood to maturity, sometimes you put your arms up and scream, sometimes you just hang on to that bar in front of you. But the ride is the thing. I think the most you can hope for at the end of life is that your hair is messed, you're out of breath, and you didn't throw up.

◆ *Jerry Seinfeld*

Live your life while you have it. Life is a splendid gift. There is nothing small in it. For the greatest things grow by God's Law out of the smallest. But to live your life you must discipline it. You must not fritter it away in "fair purpose, erring act, inconstant will" but make your thoughts, your acts, all work to the same end and that end, not self but God. That is what we call character.

◆ *Florence Nightingale*

Because of the routines we follow, we often forget that life is an ongoing adventure. We leave our homes for work, acting and even believing that we will reach our destinations with no unusual event startling us out of our set expectations. The truth is we know nothing, not where our cars will fail or when our buses will stall, whether our places of employment will be there when we arrive, or whether, in fact, we ourselves will arrive whole and alive at the end of our journeys. Life's pure adventure, and the sooner we realize that, the quicker we will be able to treat life as art: to bring all our energies to each encounter, to remain flexible enough to notice and admit when what we expected to happen did not happen. We need to remember that we are created creative and can invent new scenarios as frequently as they are needed.

Life seems to love the liver of it.

◆ *Maya Angelou*

THE WAYS OF LIFE

Life is not a road.
Life is the open sky,
Because simple choices can turn you in any direction.

Life is for better.
Life is not for worse.
Life's change is always a gift and not a curse.

Life might bring joy.
And if it brings sorrow,
Life promises us change tomorrow.

Raj Patel

The child says, "When I am a big boy." But what is that? The big boy says, "When I grow up." And then, grown up, he says, "When I get married." But to be married, what is that after all? The thought changes to "When I'm able to retire." And when retirement comes, he looks back over the landscape traversed; a cold wind seems to sweep over it; somehow he has missed it all, and it is gone. Life, we learn when it is much too late, is living and enjoying every moment of every day, whether we are ten or eighty.

Stephen Leacock

LIFE IS

Life is a challenge—meet it.
Life is a gift—accept it.
Life is an adventure—dare it.
Life is a sorrow—overcome it.
Life is a tragedy—face it.
Life is a duty—perform it.
Life is a game—play it.
Life is a mystery—unfold it.
Life is a song—sing it.
Life is an opportunity—take it.
Life is a journey—complete it.
Life is a promise—fulfill it.
Life is a beauty—praise it.
Life is a struggle—fight it.
Life is a goal—achieve it.
Life is a puzzle—solve it.
Life is eternal—believe it.

Author unknown

Life moves on, whether we act as cowards or heroes. Life has no other discipline to impose, if we would but realize it, than to accept life unquestioningly. Everything we shut our eyes to, everything we run away from, everything we deny, denigrate or despise, serves to defeat us in the end. What seems nasty, painful, evil, can become a source of beauty, joy and strength, if faced with an open mind. Every moment is a golden one for him who has the vision to recognize it as such.

◆ *Henry Miller*

What is life?
As you proceed through life,
following your own path,
birds will shit on you.
Don't bother to brush it off.

Getting a comedic view
of your situation
gives you spiritual distance.
Having a sense of humor saves you.

◆ *Joseph Campbell*

LIVING

To touch the cup with eager lips and taste, not drain it;
To woo and tempt and court a bliss—and not attain it;
To fondle and caress a joy, yet hold it lightly,

Lest it become necessity and cling too tightly;
To watch the sun set in the west without regretting;
To hail its advent in the east—the night forgetting;
To smother care in happiness and grief in laughter;
To hold the present close—not questioning hereafter;
To have enough to share—to know the joy of giving;
To thrill with all the sweets of life—is living.

Author unknown

THE BEST ADVICE

◆ ◆ ◆

It is the privilege of adults to give advice. It is the privilege of youth not to listen. Both avail themselves of their privileges, and the world rocks on.

◆ *D. Sutten*

Never allow yourself to become one of those people who, when they are old, tell you how they missed their chances.

◆ *Claire Ortega*

to be nobody—but—yourself—in a world which is doing its best, night and day, to make you everybody else—means to fight the hardest battle which any human being can fight; and never stop fighting.

◆ *e. e. cummings*

The very least you can do in your life is to figure out what you hope for. And the most you can do is live inside that hope. Not admire it from a distance but live right in it, under its roof.

◆ *Barbara Kingsolver*

You must learn day by day, year by year, to broaden your horizon. The more things you love, the more you are interested in, the more you enjoy, the more you are indignant about—the more you have left when anything happens.

◆ *Ethel Barrymore*

It's never too late to become the person you could have been.

◆ *George Eliot*

Your only obligation in any lifetime is to be true to yourself.

◆ *Richard Bach*

You can't do it all yourself. Don't be afraid to rely on others to help you accomplish your goals.

◆ *Oprah Winfrey*

People need role models at every stage of their lives . . . not just when they're kids. Don't expect a role model to come along all by him or herself. There are plenty of classy people out there who want to help. Instead of waiting for somebody to take you under their wing, go out there and find a good wing to climb under.

◆ *Dave Thomas*

Hold your head high, stick your chest out. You can make it. It gets dark sometimes but morning comes. . . . Keep hope alive.

◆ *Jesse Jackson*

When you're younger, you want to be sure that by the time you're eighty years old you can sit on the bench and look back and say, "Man, I did it all. I didn't miss a thing."

Bill Cosby

We should not let our fears hold us back from pursuing our hopes.

John F. Kennedy

It is wisdom to believe the heart.

George Santayana

I hope that my achievements in life shall be these—that I will have fought for what was right and fair, that I will have risked for that which mattered, that I will have given help to those who were in need, and that I will have left the earth a better place for what I've done and who I've been.

C. Hoppe

Dedicate yourself to the good you deserve and desire for yourself. Give yourself peace of mind. You deserve to be happy. You deserve delight.

Mark Victor Hansen

I have a simple philosophy. Fill what's empty. Empty what's full. And scratch where it itches.

Alice Roosevelt Longworth

A great man is he who does not lose his childlike heart.

Mencius

You have to leave the city of your comfort and go into the wilderness of your intuition. What you'll discover will be wonderful. What you'll discover will be yourself.

Alan Alda

Love your enemies just in case your friends turn out to be a bunch of bastards.

R. A. Dickson

Luck affects everything. Let your hook be always cast. In the stream where you least expect it, there will be a fish.

Ovid

Open up a can! The world belongs to those who say I can.

Frederick Eikerenkoetter

Do the right thing.

Spike Lee

My one piece of advice is to keep your sense of humor above all. . . . Life is, after all, essentially a joke. If you don't think so, look at the hats you're wearing.

Jeff Danziger

Enjoy yourself. These are the good old days you're going to miss in the years ahead.

Anonymous

Don't compromise yourself. You are all you've got.

Janis Joplin

This above all: to thine own self be true.

William Shakespeare

The man who graduates today and stops learning tomorrow is uneducated the day after.

Newton D. Baker

God grant me the serenity to accept the things I cannot change, the courage to change the things I can, and the wisdom to know the difference.

Reinhold Niebuhr

We can never give up the belief that the good guys always win. And that we are the good guys.

Faith Popcorn

My advice to you is not to inquire why or whither, but just to enjoy your ice cream while it's on your plate.

Thornton Wilder

Perhaps the most useful suggestion I can make, on the day when most of you are ceasing to be students, is that you go on being students for the rest of your lives. Don't move to a mental slum.

Susan Sontag

So get a few laughs and do the best you can.

Will Rogers

The best philosophy is to do one's duties, to take the world as it comes, submit respectfully to one's lot, and bless the goodness that has given us so much happiness with it, whatever it is.

Horace Walpole

As you walk and eat and travel, be where you are. Otherwise you will miss most of your life.

Buddha

Love your enemies. It makes them so damned mad.

P. D. East

It is not how much we have, but how much we enjoy, that makes happiness.

Charles H. Spurgeon

Remember that you are all people and that all people are you.

Joy Harjo

As simple as it sounds, we all must try to be the best person we can: by making the best choices, by making the most of the talents we've been given.

Mary Lou Retton

Love doesn't make the world go round. Love is what makes the ride worthwhile.

Franklin P. Jones

Don't look for a lover. Be one.

James Leo Herlihy

Part of being a champ is acting like a champ. You have to learn how to win and not run away when you lose. . . . Everyone has bad stretches and real successes. Either way, you have to be careful not to lose your confidence or get too confident.

Nancy Kerrigan

Beginning today, treat everyone you meet as if they were going to be dead by midnight. Extend to them all the care, kindness and understanding you can muster, and do it with no thought of any reward. Your life will never be the same again.

Og Mandino

Choose Love, Love!
Without the sweet life of Love,
living is a burden—as you have seen.

◆ *Rumi*

So whatever you do, just do it. Do not worry about making a fool of yourself. Making a damn fool of yourself is absolutely essential. And you will have a great time.

◆ *Gloria Steinem*

Carpe diem, quam minimum credula postero.
(Seize the day and put as little trust as you can in tomorrow.)

◆ *Horace*

Anyone who stops learning is old, whether at twenty or eighty. Anyone who keeps learning stays young. The greatest thing in life is to keep your mind young.

◆ *Henry Ford*

Leave nothing undone which ought to be done; do nothing which ought to be omitted. Let the transitory vanities, the visionary enjoyments of time fleet by you, unnoticed. Point all of your views to the elevated scenes of an immortal existence, and remember that this life is but the dawn of your being.

◆ *Timothy Dwight*

Try not to become a man of success but rather try to become a man of value.

              ◆ *Albert Einstein*

Keep walking and keep smiling.

              ◆ *Tiny Tim*

1. Be discoverers.
2. Be ready helpers.
3. Be friend makers.

              ◆ *The Brownie "B's" (Girl Scouts)*

When you go out into this world, remember: compassion, compassion, compassion.

              ◆ *Betty Williams*

There are no rules. Just follow your heart.

              ◆ *Robin Williams*

Just be what you are and speak from your guts and heart—it's all a man has.

              ◆ *Hubert H. Humphrey*

The best advice I can give to any young man or young woman upon graduation from school can be summed up in exactly eight words: Be honest with yourself and tell the truth.

James A. Farley

I've always believed that you can think positive just as well as you can think negative.

Sugar Ray Robinson

Everything is practice.

Pele

What counts is not necessarily the size of the dog in the fight, but the size of the fight in the dog.

Dwight D. Eisenhower

Keep away from people who try to belittle your ambitions. Small people always do that, but the really great make you feel that you, too, can become great.

Mark Twain

Don't hurry. Don't worry. You're only here on a short visit, so don't forget to stop and smell the flowers.

Walter Hagan

Wealth should never be your goal in life. True wealth is of the heart, not of the purse. . . . Do not aspire for wealth and labor only to be rich. Strive instead for happiness, to be loved and to love, and most important, to acquire peace of mind and serenity.

◆ *Og Mandino*

You will do foolish things, but do them with enthusiasm.

◆ *Colette*

If I were asked to give what I consider the single most useful bit of advice for all humanity it would be this: Expect trouble as an inevitable part of life and when it comes, hold your head high, look it squarely in the eye and say, "I will be bigger than you. You cannot defeat me."

◆ *Ann Landers*

Speak softly and carry a big stick; you will go far.

◆ *Theodore Roosevelt*

Speaking to you today marks a milestone in my life. I am forty years old. Twenty-two years ago, when I was in your seat, I never, ever thought I would be forty years old.

The implications of being your speaker frighten me. For one thing, when a forty-year-old geezer spoke at my baccalaureate ceremony, he was about the last person I'd believe. I have no intention of giving you the boring speech that you are dreading. This speech will be short, sweet, and not boring.

I am going to talk about hindsights today. Hindsights that I've accumulated in the twenty years from where you are to where I am. Don't blindly believe me. Don't take what I say as "truth." Just listen. Perhaps my experience can help you out a tiny bit.

I will present them à la David Letterman. Yes, forty-year-old people can still stay up past eleven.

#10: Live off your parents as long as possible.

When I spoke at this ceremony two years ago, this was the most popular hindsight—except from the point of view of the parents. Thus, I knew I was on the right track.

I was a diligent Oriental in high school and college. I took college-level classes and earned college-level credits. I rushed through college in three and a half years. I never traveled or took time off because I thought it wouldn't prepare me for work and it would delay my graduation.

Frankly, I blew it.

You are going to work the rest of your lives, so don't be in a rush to start. Stretch out your college education. Now is the time to suck life into your lungs—before you have a mortgage, kids, and car payments.

Take whole semesters off to travel overseas. Take jobs and internships that pay less money or no money. Investigate your passions on your parents' nickel. Or dime. Or quarter. Or dollar. Your goal should be to extend college to at least six years.

Delay, as long as possible, the inevitable entry into the workplace and a lifetime of servitude to bozos who know less than you do, but who make more money. Also, you shouldn't deprive your parents of the pleasure of supporting you.

#9 *Pursue joy, not happiness.*

This is probably the hardest lesson of all to learn. It probably seems to you that the goal in life is to be "happy." Oh, you may have to sacrifice and study and work hard, but, by and large, happiness should be predictable.

Nice house. Nice car. Nice material things.

Take my word for it, happiness is temporary and fleeting. Joy, by contrast, is unpredictable. It comes from pursuing interests and passions that do not *obviously* result in happiness.

Pursuing joy, not happiness will translate into one thing over the next few years for you: *Study what you love.* This may also not be popular with parents. When I went to college, I was "market driven." It's also an Oriental thing.

I looked at what fields had the greatest job opportunities and prepared myself for them. This was brain dead. There are so many ways to make a living in the world, it doesn't matter that you've taken all the "right" courses. I don't think one person on the original Macintosh team had a classic "computer science" degree.

You parents have a responsibility in this area. Don't force your kids to follow in your footsteps or to live your dreams. My father was a senator in Hawaii. His dream was to be a lawyer, but he only had a high school education. He wanted me to be a lawyer.

For him, I went to law school. For me, I quit after two weeks. I view this as a terrific validation of my inherent intelligence.

#8: *Challenge the known and embrace the unknown.*

One of the biggest mistakes you can make in life is to accept the known and resist the unknown. You should, in fact, do exactly the opposite: challenge the known and embrace the unknown.

Let me tell you a short story about ice. In the late 1800s there was a thriving ice industry in the Northeast. Companies would cut blocks of ice from frozen lakes and ponds and sell them around the world. The largest single shipment was two hundred tons that was shipped to India. One hundred tons got there unmelted, but this was enough to make a profit.

These ice harvesters, however, were put out of business by companies that invented mechanical ice makers. It was no longer necessary to cut and ship ice because companies could make it in any city during any season.

These ice makers, however, were put out of business by refrigerator companies. If it was convenient to make ice at a manufacturing plant, imagine how much better it was to make ice and create cold storage in everyone's home.

You would think that the ice harvesters would have seen the advantages of ice making and adopted this technology. However, all they could think about was the known: better saws, better storage, better transportation.

Then you would think that the ice makers would have seen the advantages of refrigerators and adopted this technology. The truth is that the ice harvesters couldn't embrace the unknown and jump their curve to the next curve.

Challenge the known and embrace the unknown, or you'll be like the ice harvesters and ice makers.

#7: *Learn to speak a foreign language, play a musical instrument, and play noncontact sports.*

Learn a foreign language. I studied Latin in high school because I thought it would help me increase my vocabulary. It did, but trust me when I tell you it's very difficult to have a conversation in Latin today other than at the Vatican. And despite all my efforts, the Pope has yet to call for my advice.

Learn to play a musical instrument. My only connection to music today is that I was named after Guy Lombardo. Trust me: it's better than being named after Guy's brother, Carmen. Playing a musical instrument could be with me now and stay with me forever. Instead, I have to buy CDs at Tower.

I played football. I loved football. Football is macho. I was a middle linebacker—arguably one of the most macho positions in a macho game. But you should also learn to play a noncontact sport like basketball or tennis. That is, a sport you can play when you're over the hill.

It will be as difficult when you're forty to get twenty-two guys together in a stadium to play football as it is to have a conversation in Latin, but all the people who wore cute white tennis outfits can still play tennis. And all the macho football players are sitting around watching television and drinking beer.

#6: Continue to learn.

Learning is a process not an event. I thought learning would be over when I got my degree. It's not true. You should never stop learning. Indeed, it gets easier to learn once you're out of school because it's easier to see the relevance of why you need to learn.

You're learning in a structured, dedicated environment right now. On your parents' nickel. But don't confuse "school" and "learning." You can go to school and not learn a thing. You can also learn a tremendous amount without school.

#5: Learn to like yourself or change yourself until you can like yourself.

I know a forty-year-old woman who was a drug addict. She is a mother of three. She traced the start of her drug addiction to smoking dope in high school.

I'm not going to lecture you about not taking drugs. Hey, I smoked dope in high school. Unlike Bill Clinton, I inhaled. Also unlike Bill Clinton, I exhaled.

This woman told me that she started taking drugs because she hated herself when she was sober. She did not like drugs as much as she hated herself. Drugs were not the cause, though she thought they were the solution.

She turned her life around only after she realized that she was in a downward spiral. Fix your problem. Fix your life. Then you won't need to take drugs. Drugs are neither the solution nor the problem.

Frankly, smoking, drugs, alcohol—and using an IBM PC—are signs of stupidity. End of discussion.

#4: Don't get married too soon.

I got married when I was thirty-two. That's about the right age. Until you're about that age, you may not know who you are. You also may not know who you're marrying.

I don't know one person who got married too late. I know many people who got married too young. If you do decide to get married, just keep in mind that you need to accept the person for what he or she is right now.

#3: Play to win and win to play.

Playing to win is one of the finest things you can do. It enables you to fulfill your potential. It enables you to improve the world and, conveniently, develop high expectations for everyone else too.

And what if you lose? Just make sure you lose while trying something grand. Avinash Dixit, an economics professor at Princeton, and Barry Nalebuff, an economics and management professor at the Yale School of Organization and Management, say it this way: "If you are going to fail, you might as well fail at a difficult task. Failure causes others to downgrade their expectations of you in the future. The seriousness of this problem depends on what you attempt."

In its purest form, winning becomes a means, not an end, to improve yourself and your competition.

Winning is also a means to play again. The unexamined life may not be worth living, but the unlived life is not worth examining. The rewards of winning—money, power, satisfaction, and self-confidence—should not be squandered.

Thus, in addition to playing to win, you have a second, more important obligation: To compete again to the depth and breadth and height that your soul can reach. Ultimately, your greatest competition is yourself.

#2: Obey the absolutes.

Playing to win, however, does not mean playing dirty. As you grow older and older, you will find that things change from absolute to relative. When you were very young, it was absolutely wrong to lie, cheat, or steal.

As you get older, and particularly when you enter the workforce, you will be tempted by the "system" to think in relative terms. "I made more money." "I have a nicer car." "I went on a better vacation."

Worse, "I didn't cheat as much on my taxes as my partner." "I just have a few drinks. I don't take cocaine." "I don't pad my expense reports as much as others."

This is completely wrong. Preserve and obey the absolutes as much as you can. If you never lie, cheat, or steal, you will never have to remember who you lied to, how you cheated, and what you stole.

There absolutely are absolute rights and wrongs.

#1: *Enjoy your family and friends before they are gone.*

This is the most important hindsight. It doesn't need much explanation. I'll just repeat it: Enjoy your family and friends before they are gone.

Nothing—not money, power, or fame—can replace your family and friends or bring them back once they are gone. Our greatest joy has been our baby, and I predict that children will bring you the greatest joy in your lives—especially if they graduate from college in four years.

And now, I'm going to give you one extra hindsight because I've probably cost your parents thousands of dollars today. It's something that I hate to admit too.

By and large, the older you get, the more you're going to realize that your parents were right. More and more—until finally, you become your parents. I know you're all saying, "Yeah, right." Mark my words.

Remember these ten things: if just one of them helps just one of you, this speech will have been a success:

#10: Live off your parents as long as possible.
#9: Pursue joy, not happiness.
#8: Challenge the known and embrace the unknown.
#7: Learn to speak a foreign language, play a musical instrument, and play noncontact sports.

#6: Continue to learn.

#5: Learn to like yourself or change yourself until you can like yourself.

#4: Don't get married too soon.

#3: Play to win and win to play.

#2: Obey the absolutes.

#1: Enjoy your family and friends before they are gone.

Congratulations on your graduation. Thank you very much.

Guy Kawasaki

Today you meet to say good-bye to the past, and to begin a new and very personal journey—to search for your own true colors. In the world that awaits you beyond this school, no one can say what your true colors will be. But this I do know: You have a first-class education from a first-class school. And so you need not, probably cannot, live a "paint-by-numbers" life. Decisions are not irrevocable. Choices do come back. As you set off from here, I hope that many of you will consider making three very special choices.

The first is to believe in something larger than yourself, to get involved in some of the big ideas of your time. I chose literacy because I honestly believe that if more people could read, write and comprehend, we would be that much closer to solving so many of the problems plaguing our society.

Early on I made another choice which I hope you will make as well.

Whether you are talking about education, career, or service, you are talking about life, and life must have joy. It's supposed to be fun! One of the reasons I made the most important decision of my life, to marry George Bush, is because he made me laugh. It's true—sometimes we've laughed through our tears, but that shared laughter has been one of our strongest bonds. Find the joy in life, because as Ferris Bueller said on his day off, "Life moves pretty fast. Ya don't stop and look around once in a while, ya gonna miss it!"

The third choice that must not be missed is to cherish your human connections: your relationships with friends and family. For several years, you've had impressed upon you the importance to your career of dedication and hard work. This is true, but as important as your obligations as a doctor, lawyer or business leader will be, you are a human being first and those human connections—with spouses, with children, with friends—are the most important investments you will ever make. At the end of your life, you will never regret not having passed one more test, not winning one more verdict or not closing one more deal. You will regret time not spent with a husband, a friend, a child or a parent.

◆ *Barbara Bush*

I have an everyday religion that works for me: Love yourself first and everything else falls into line. You really have to love yourself to get anything done in this world.

◆ *Lucille Ball*

IF

If you can keep your head when all about you
Are losing theirs and blaming it on you;
If you can trust yourself when all men doubt you,
But make allowance for their doubting too;
If you can wait and not be tired by waiting,
Or, being lied about, don't deal in lies,
Or, being hated, don't give way to hating,
And yet don't look too good, nor talk too wise;

If you can dream—and not make dreams your master;
If you can think—and not make thoughts your aim;
If you can meet with triumph and disaster
And treat those two impostors just the same;
If you can bear to hear the truth you've spoken
Twisted by knaves to make a trap for fools,
Or watch the things you gave your life to broken,
And stoop and build 'em up with worn-out tools;

If you can make one heap of all your winnings
And risk it on one turn of pitch-and-toss,
And lose, and start again at your beginnings
And never breathe a word about your loss;
If you can force your heart and nerve and sinew
To serve your turn long after they are gone,

And so hold on when there is nothing in you
Except the Will which says to them: "Hold on";

If you can talk with crowds and keep your virtue,
Or walk with kings—nor lose the common touch;
If neither foes nor loving friends can hurt you;
If all men count with you, but none too much;
If you can fill the unforgiving minute
With sixty seconds' worth of distance run—
Yours is the Earth and everything that's in it,
And—which is more—you'll be a Man my son!

◆ *Rudyard Kipling*

The important thing is not to stop questioning. Curiosity has its own reason for existing. One cannot help but be in awe when he contemplates the mysteries of eternity, of life, of the marvelous structure of reality. It is enough if one tried merely to comprehend a little of this mystery every day. Never lose a holy curiosity.

◆ *Albert Einstein*

If you fall, boy, you don't have to wallow. Ain't nobody going to think you somebody unless you think so yourself. Don't listen to their talk, boy, they don't have a pot to pee in or a window to throw it out. For God's sake, Jesse, promise me you'll be somebody. Ain't no such thing as "cain't," "cain't" got drowned in a soda bottle. Don't let the Joneses get you down. Nothing is impossible for those who love the

Lord. Come hell or high water, if you got guts, boy, ain't nothing or nobody can turn you around.

Matilda Burns
(Jesse Jackson's grandmother)

JOHN WESLEY'S RULE

Do all the good you can,
By all the means you can,
In all the ways you can,
In all the places you can,
At all the times you can,
To all the people you can,
As long as you ever can.

BE

Be understanding to your enemies.
Be loyal to your friends.
Be strong enough to face the world each day.
Be weak enough to know you cannot do everything alone.
Be generous to those who need your help.
Be frugal with what you need yourself.
Be wise enough to know that you do not know everything.
Be foolish enough to believe in miracles.
Be willing to share your joys.

Be willing to share the sorrows of others.
Be a leader when you see a path others have missed.
Be a follower when you are shrouded by the mists of uncertainty.
Be the first to congratulate an opponent who succeeds.
Be the last to criticize a colleague who fails.
Be sure where your next step will fall, so that you will not stumble.
Be sure of your final destination, in case you are going the wrong way.
Be loving to those who love you.
Be loving to those who do not love you, and they may change.
Above all, be yourself.

Author unknown

MATURITY

Maturity is the ability to control anger and settle differences without violence or destruction.

Maturity is patience. It is the willingness to pass up immediate pleasure in favor of the long-term gain.

Maturity is perseverance, the ability to sweat out a project or a situation in spite of heavy opposition and discouraging setbacks.

Maturity is the capacity to face unpleasantness and frustration, discomfort and defeat, without complaint or collapse.

Maturity is humility. It is being big enough to say, "I was wrong." And, when right, the mature person need not experience the satisfaction of saying, "I told you so."

Maturity is the ability to make a decision and stand by it. The immature spend their lives exploring endless possibilities; then they do nothing.

Maturity means dependability, keeping one's word, coming through in a crisis. The immature are masters of the alibi. They are the confused and the disorganized. Their lives are a maze of broken promises, former friends, unfinished business and good intentions that somehow never materialize.

Maturity is the art of living in peace with that which we cannot change, the courage to change that which should be changed and the wisdom to know the difference.

Author unknown

I think everyone is unique. We know that. The only way you find out what you are is by trying everything, and then at some point you take what you are, which is unique. Don't ever try to mimic anybody, because you will only be second best. You can never outshine the thing you are trying to mimic, so don't ever do that. Don't idol worship. Finally, be yourself. Then you are going to be really unique and exciting. People are going to beat a path to your door if you polish your inner self.

Robert D. Ballard

Nine requisites for contented living: Health enough to make work a pleasure. Wealth enough to support your needs. Strength to battle with difficulties and overcome them. Grace enough to confess your sins and forsake them. Patience enough to toil until some good is accomplished. Charity enough to see some good in your neighbor. Love enough to move you to be useful and helpful to others. Faith enough to make real the things of God. Hope enough to remove all anxious fears concerning the future.

◆ *Johann von Goethe*

I think that education is power. I think that being able to communicate with people is power. One of my main goals on the planet is to encourage people to empower themselves. I do that through my work on television and my work socially with organizations and my work in my relationships. I do think that the greatest lesson of life is that you are responsible for your own life.

◆ *Oprah Winfrey*

Continue searching harder, deeper, faster, stronger, and louder and knowing that one day you'll be called upon to use all that you've amassed in the process. With that wealth of self-knowledge, you hold all of our futures in your hands. So you better make it good. You better keep your eyes open and your hearts open and find out what's beneath the surface. What moves you, what repels you, and what compels you. Become human first and identify what exactly that is later. Let how you live your life stand for something, no matter how small and incidental it may seem. Because it's not good enough to put change in the meter without questioning what the meter's doing there in the first place. It's not good enough to let life pass you by in the name of some greater glory. This is it. This is all you get. So love this life, curse this life, and claim this life for your very own.

◆ *Jodie Foster*

Yesterday is a canceled check;
tomorrow is a promissory note;
today is the only cash you have—so
spend it wisely.

◆ *Kay Lyons*

CHANGING THE WORLD

When I was a young man, I wanted to change the world. I found it was difficult to change the world, so I tried to change my nation. When I found I couldn't change the nation, I began to focus on my town. I couldn't change the town, and as an older man, I tried to change my family. Now, as an old man, I realize the only thing I can change is myself, and suddenly I realize that if long ago I had changed myself, I could have made an impact on my family. My family and I could have made an impact on our town. Their impact could have changed the nation and I could indeed have changed the world.

◆ *Unknown monk, A.D. 1100*

People's lives change. To keep all your old friends is like keeping all your old clothes—pretty soon your closet is so jammed and everything so crushed you can't find anything to wear. Help these friends when they need you; bless the years and happy times when you meant a lot to each other, but try not to have the guilts if new people mean more to you now.

◆ *Helen Gurley Brown*

Most of the time you are growing up, people tell you what's wrong with you. Your coach tells you, your parents tell you, the teachers tell you when they grade you. I think that that's good in the early stages, because it helps you then develop skills. But at some point in your career, generally I think when you are in your teens, you look in a mirror and you have to say, despite all the bumps and warts, "I like that person I'm looking at, and let's just do our best."

◆ *Robert D. Ballard*

First I was dying to finish high school and start college.
And then I was dying to finish college and start working.
And then I was dying to marry and have children.
And then I was dying for my children to grow old enough so I could
    return to work.
And then I was dying to retire.
And now, I am dying . . . and suddenly realize *I forgot to live.*

◆ *Anonymous*

There's no such thing as failure. Mistakes happen in your life to bring into focus more clearly who you really are. Trials happen in your life. . . . What really matters is how much truth you can bring to your life, how much integrity, how much generosity, how much forgiveness, how much love. I wish heaven for you. I expect that you will do great work, that you will be great and that your life will be blessed. God bless you all.

Oprah Winfrey

Watch your thoughts; they become words.
Watch your words; they become actions.
Watch your actions; they become habits.
Watch your habits; they become character.
Watch your character; it becomes your destiny.

Frank Outlaw

Join the great company of those who make barren places of life fruitful with kindness. Carry a vision of heaven in your souls and you shall make the world correspond to that vision.

External conditions are the accidents of life, its outer trappings. The great enduring realities are love of service. Joy is the holy fire that keeps our purpose warm and our intelligence aglow. Resolve to keep happy and your joy and you shall form an invincible host against difficulty.

Helen Keller

Count your garden by the flowers
Never by the leaves that fall;
Count your days by the golden hours,
Don't remember clouds at all.
Count the nights by stars, not shadows,
Count your life by smiles, not tears,
And with joy on every birthday
Count your age by friends, not years.

Anonymous

Each of us has the right and the responsibility to assess the roads which lie ahead, and those over which we have traveled, and if the future road looms ominous or unpromising, and the roads back uninviting, then we need to gather our resolve and, carrying only the necessary baggage, step off that road into another direction.

Maya Angelou

If you want happiness for an hour—take a nap.
If you want happiness for a day—go fishing.
If you want happiness for a month—get married.
If you want happiness for a year—inherit a fortune.
If you want happiness for a lifetime—help others.

Chinese proverb

This game . . . it's a big wheel. It goes around in a circle. Sometimes you're at the top. Sometimes you're in the middle. Sometimes you're at the bottom. Sometimes you stay a little too much at the bottom. But you know you're going to be at the top again. Everybody will have his opportunities.

◆ *Jose Santos*

This is what you shall do: Love the earth and sun and the animals, despise riches, give alms to every one that asks, stand up for the stupid and crazy, devote your income and labor to others, hate tyrants, argue not concerning God, have patience and indulgence toward the people, take off your hat to nothing known or unknown or to any man or number of men, go freely with powerful uneducated persons and with the young and with the mothers of families, read these leaves in the open air every season of every year of your life, re-examine all you have been told at school or church or in any book, dismiss whatever insults your own soul, and your very flesh shall be a great poem and have the richest fluency not only in its words but in the silent lines of its lips and face and between the lashes of your eyes and in every motion and joint of your body.

◆ *Walt Whitman*

A lot of people have been quoting me ever since I came to play for the Yankees in 1946. But, as I once said, I really didn't say everything I said. So now it's my turn to give some of my famous advice to the graduates. First, never give up, because it's never over till it's over. Second, during the years ahead, when you come to a fork in the road, take it. Third, don't always follow the crowd, because nobody goes there anymore. It's too crowded. Fourth, stay alert. You can observe a lot by watching. Fifth, and last, remember that whatever you do in life, 90 percent of it is half mental.

◆ *Yogi Berra*

Do not worry, eat three square meals a day, say your prayers, be courteous to your creditors, keep your digestion good, steer clear of biliousness, exercise, go slow and go easy. Maybe there are other things that your special case requires to make you happy, but, my friend, these I reckon will give you a good lift.

◆ *Abraham Lincoln*

You are no longer tadpoles. The time has come for you to leave the swamp. But I am sure that wherever I go as I travel around the world, I will find each and every one of you working your tails off to save other swamps and give those of us who live there a chance to survive. . . . May success and a smile always be yours, even when you are knee-deep in the sticky mud of life.

◆ *Kermit the Frog*

The advice I would give any young person is, first of all, to rid themselves of prejudice against other people and to be concerned about what they can do to help others. And of course, to get a good education, and take advantage of the opportunities that they have. In fact, there are more opportunities today than when I was young. And whatever they do, to think positively and be concerned about other people, to think in terms of them being able to not succumb to many of the temptations, especially the use of drugs and substances that will destroy the physical health, as well as mental health.

◆ *Rosa Parks*

To live content with small means; to seek elegance rather than luxury; and refinement rather than fashion; to be worthy, not respectable; and wealthy, not rich; to study hard, think quietly, talk gently, act frankly; to listen to stars and birds, to babes and sages, with open heart; to bear all cheerfully, do all bravely, await occasion, hurry never; in a word, to let the spiritual, unbidden and unconscious grow up through the common. This is to be my symphony.

◆ *William Henry Channing*

you shall above all things be glad and young.
for if you're young, whatever life you wear

it will become you; and if you are glad
whatever's living will yourself become.

◆ *e. e. cummings*

THE WORLD IS WAITING FOR YOU

The world is waiting for you, young man,
    If your purpose is strong and true;

If out of your treasures of mind and heart,
    You can bring things old and new,
If you know the truth that makes men free,
    And with skill can bring it to view,
The world is waiting for you, young man,
    The world is waiting for you.

There are treasures of mountain and treasures of sea,
    And halves of valley and plain,
That Industry, Knowledge and Skill can secure,
    While Ignorance wishes in vain.
To scatter the lightning and harness the storm,
    Is a power that is wielded by few;
If you have the nerve and the skill, young man,
    The world is waiting for you.

Of the idle and brainless the world has enough—
    Who eat what they never have earned;
Who hate the pure stream from the fountain of truth,
    And wisdom and knowledge have spurned.
But patience and purpose which know no defeat,
    And genius like gems bright and true,
Will bless all mankind with their love, life and light,—
    The world is waiting for you.

Then awake, O young man, from the stupor of doubt,
    And prepare for the battle of life,

Be the fire of the forge, or be anvil or sledge,—
    But win, or go down in the strife—
Can you stand though the world into ruin should rock?
    Can you conquer with many or few?
Then the world is waiting for you, young man,
    The world is waiting for you!

◆ *Prof. S. S. Calkins*

If I were to give advice to young people, high-achieving young people for example, I'd have to say, don't neglect your family. Politics is important, sitting at the head table is glamorous. Traveling around the world, trying to do something for world peace was wonderful. But . . . family and friends and faith are what are really matters in life. And I know that. I see it so clearly now.

◆ *George Bush*

Be sensitive in every way possible about everything in life. Be sensitive. Insensitivity brings indifference and nothing is worse than indifference. Indifference makes that person dead before the person dies. Indifference means there is a kind of apathy that sets in and you no longer appreciate beauty, friendship, goodness, or anything. So, therefore, do not be insensitive. Be sensitive, only sensitive. Of course it hurts. Sensitivity is painful. So what. Think of those that you have to be sensitive to. Their pain is greater than yours.

◆ *Elie Wiesel*

"I thought the tassel looked a little bland
so I had it permed."

Lord, make me an instrument of Thy peace.
Where there is hatred, let me sow love;
where there is injury, pardon;
where there is doubt, faith;
where there is despair, hope;
where there is sadness, joy;
where there is darkness, light.

O Divine Master,
grant that I may not so much seek to be consoled, as to console;
not so much to be understood, as to understand;
not so much to be loved, as to love.
For it is in giving that we receive,
it is in pardoning that we are pardoned,
it is in dying that we are born again to eternal life.

◆ *St. Francis of Assisi*

My Sons and Daughters in Spirit:

We are all very proud of you. Four years ago, you arrived as new citizens to this campus. You were wet behind the ears, and the time stretched before you, I think, when you came in as seeming infinity. In retrospect, the years have vanished in a snap. It took a lot of commitment, I think, to stick it out, to buckle down, to do things you really didn't want to do: like exams, or papers, or research. It took a lot of growing up to get through the heartache or maybe even the homesickness some of you may have felt. But you've done it, and I think you should be very proud of your accomplishment. I know all of us are.

And I know too that we do have concern for you in today's world. When I was leaving college, the world was quite a different place, not so fast. I lived through the Beat Generation, and the Flower Child and feminist eras, and the hippies, and the Me Generation, and the Yuppies, and now Generation X and Grunge. What will you live through? What moniker will be hung on you in the next ten years or so? Well I hope it will symbolize the "I care" generation, because I know a lot of people your age, and I know you do care.

I have great faith in you. You are alive and young and well educated at a remarkable time in world history. You are well informed and you can surf the Web when others of us just kind of wade in the shallows. You actually know how big a megabyte is! You've seen the prospect of peace in the Middle East, and the ceasefire in Bosnia, and the Beatles' Reunion (well, sort of).

What we ask, sons and daughters, for the years of room and board with Mom and Dad, what we ask is that as you become working citizens of the community, the state and the country, that you take very good care of this world that you're inheriting for the twenty-first century.

As your parents, we have cared for you; as your teachers and friends, we have cared, and we ask that you do so as well. Take care of our environment, our natural resources. This is one planet that we inhabit together, and it is finite. We must keep Mother Earth whole and healthy.

Care about the legacy that you leave behind. After all, when we think of places that we have loved, we remember mostly three things: we remember the natural beauty, the people and the cultural stamp of the place. Long after wars are won or lost, art and science endure. Our cultural legacy tells the next generation about the people who lived then and there—how expansive they were or how prosaic. Great people leave a great testament: beautifully designed buildings, enduring stories in books or on film, timeless visual art and the legends of the ephemeral performing arts.

Lastly, care about your fellow human beings. It is simply not good enough when the greatest nation in the world steps over the ill and the destitute. It is not good enough that one child goes to bed hungry or bruised or uneducated. It is not good enough when we exclude anyone who is different from ourselves. An indignity suffered by anyone is our indignity as well.

Others have cared for you. Now, sons and daughters, it is your turn. And so, friends, children, I congratulate you on this day for all you have achieved and for the promise that is vested in each and every one of you. May life be all that you make it.

◆ *Jane Alexander*

DREAMS OF THE FUTURE

◆ ◆ ◆

Do you dream big? You are only limited by your dreams! Hard work is the key to success. There is a price to pay for everything. Are you prepared to pay it?

◆ *Tiger Woods*

Faith and hope are the antidote. Stay actively involved in manifesting your dreams and the world created will be one we all want to live in.

◆ *Jewel Kilcher*

I want to tell you—all you kids here and all you kids at home—that you can live your dreams if you keep believing in yourself.

◆ *Rosie O'Donnell*

For over the years I have learned that life is a voyage of discovery and not a safe harbor. It is on the voyage that we learn how to steer our own lives and with them the life of the nation we love. We learn to coexist with our fears, to surmount the obstacles before us. We find ways to defy danger, even as we reach deep within ourselves for solutions to the challenges of the age. Today, you lay claim to the future. You take a step—nothing more, nothing less—toward making that future your own. But what a step! And what a future beckons. Remember the pearl inside the oyster. Remember the lessons imparted here. Most of all, remember and revere the investment of love made over many years by parents, teachers, and friends—all of them handing you the baton and wishing you well in the ongoing race of life.

◆ *Katherine D. Ortega*

Dare to err and to dream. Deep meaning often lies in childish plays.

◆ *Johann Friedrich von Schiller*

You cannot be wimpy out there on the dream-seeking trail. Dare to break through barriers, to find your own path.

◆ *Les Brown*

To dream anything that you want to dream, that is the beauty of the human mind. To do anything that you want to do, that is the strength of the human will. To trust yourself, to test your limits, that is the courage to succeed.

◆ *Bernard Edmonds*

The greatest waste in the world is the difference between what we are and what we could become.

Ben Herbster

From then on, the boy understood his heart. He asked it, please, never to stop speaking to him. He asked that, when he wandered far from his dreams, his heart press him and sound the alarm. The boy swore that, every time he heard the alarm, he would heed its message.

Paulo Coelho

There is no Eden or heavenly gates
That you're gonna make it to one day
But all of the answers you seek can be found
In the dreams that you dream on the way.

Dan Fogelberg

Hope is the pillar that holds up the world. Hope is the dream of a waking man.

Pliny the Elder

When we can't dream any longer, we die.

Emma Goldman

If you really want something you can figure out how to make it happen.

Cher

Dreams do come true, if we only wish hard enough. You can have anything in life if you will sacrifice everything else for it.

◆ *Sir James M. Barrie*

No person has the right to rain on your dreams.

◆ *Marian Wright Edelman*

Keep true to the dreams of your youth.

◆ *Johann Friedrich von Schiller*

If you don't have a dream, how are you going to make a dream come true?

◆ *Oscar Hammerstein*

Don't be afraid of the space between your dreams and reality. If you can dream it, you can make it so.

◆ *Belva Davis*

Nothing is as real as a dream. The world can change around you, but your dream will not. Responsibilities need not erase it. Duties need not obscure it. Because the dream is within you, no one can take it away.

◆ *Tom Clancy*

The moment of enlightenment is when a person's dreams of possibilities become images of probabilities.

◆ *Vic Braden*

I have heard it said that the first ingredient of success—the earliest spark in the dreaming youth—is this; dream a great dream.

◆ *John A. Appleman*

May your future be worthy of your dreams.

◆ *Barbara Bush*

As you pursue your grand dreams, never forget the person you really want to be. More vital than success at work or in personal pursuits is the character that you will develop in the process. On a very deep level you will seek to be the kind of person that enjoys wholesome self-respect.

◆ *Robert H. Schuller*

Saddle your dreams afore you ride 'em.

◆ *Mary Webb*

To dream, it takes work. To have a nightmare takes nothing. I think if you are going to dream, you've got to be willing to work, because then it can be possible. If you are going to have a nightmare, you don't have to do anything but just hide in the closet. And I say dreams are possible through a lot of hard work.

◆ *Herschel Walker*

A dreamer is one who can only find his way by moonlight, and his punishment is that he sees the dawn before the rest of the world.

Oscar Wilde

For glory gives herself only to those who have always dreamed of her.

Charles de Gaulle

Dream no small dreams. They have no power to stir the souls of men.

Victor Hugo

The future belongs to those who believe in the beauty of their dreams.

Eleanor Roosevelt

I used to work at the International House of Pancakes. It was a dream, and I made it happen.

Paula Poundstone

I have had dreams, and I have had nightmares. I overcame the nightmares because of my dreams.

Jonas Salk

It is difficult to say what is impossible, for the dream of yesterday is the hope of today and the reality of tomorrow.

Robert H. Goddard

You can make a difference. You can change the world. Because you are the difference. You are the world.

◆ *Federico Peña*

If one advances confidently in the direction of his dreams, and endeavors to live the life which he has imagined, he will meet with a success unexpected in common hours.

◆ *Henry David Thoreau*

The thing you have to be prepared for is that other people don't always dream your dream.

◆ *Linda Ronstadt*

I like the dreams for the future better than the history of the past.

◆ *Thomas Jefferson*

We can do whatever we wish to do provided our wish is strong enough. . . . What do you want most to do? That's what I have to keep asking myself, in the face of difficulties.

◆ *Katherine Mansfield*

The truth is, pursuing a Big Dream of our own choosing is the same amount of work as gathering more and more of the things we don't really want. You're going to spend the rest of your life doing something. It might as well be something you want to do.

◆ *John-Roger & Peter McWilliams*

It is the greatest shot of adrenaline to be doing what you've wanted to do so badly. You almost feel like you could fly without the plane.

Charles Lindbergh

The poor man is not he who is without a cent, but he who is without a dream.

Harry Kemp

Nothing happens unless first a dream.

Carl Sandburg

Each of us should make the most of our lives. We should give life our best—let us use our lives more wisely to chase our dreams, find our true purpose, and be as happy and successful as possible.

Malcolm X

We grow through our dreams. All great men and women are dreamers. Some, however, allow their dreams to die. You should nurse your dreams and protect them through bad times and tough times to the sunshine and light which always come through.

Woodrow Wilson

People with dreams know no poverty. Each of us is as rich as our own dreams.

Benjamin E. Mays

When I look at the future, it's so bright, it burns my eyes.

Oprah Winfrey

The successful man or woman has a guiding vision, a dream, a sense of focus. He or she has a clear idea of what he or she wants to have, do, or accomplish. It is the achiever's divine right to dream.

Dennis Kimbro

Having a dream isn't stupid, Norm. It's not having a dream that's stupid.

Cliff Clavin (TV show *Cheers*)

You have to have a dream so you can get up in the morning.

Billy Wilder

The angel said that all the world needed was an example. People who were capable of following their dreams and of fighting for their ideas.

Paulo Coehlo

Happiness comes only when we push our brains and hearts to the farthest reaches of which we are capable.

Leo C. Rosten

Cherish your visions and your dreams, as they are the children of your soul; the blueprints of your ultimate achievements.

Napoleon Hill

We should show life neither as it is or as it ought to be, but only as we see it in our dreams.

◆ *Leo Tolstoy*

Dream lofty dreams, and as you dream, so shall you become. Your vision is the promise of what you shall at last reveal.

◆ *John Ruskin*

Dream as if you'll live forever. Live as if you'll die tomorrow.

◆ *James Dean*

Feeding a fire within you—living *for* a dream—is *real* living.

◆ *Les Brown*

Dream the dream onward.

◆ *Carl Jung*

We all have dreams. But in order to make dreams into reality, it takes an awful lot of determination, dedication, self-discipline, and effort.

◆ *Jesse Owens*

If you can dream it, you can do it.

◆ *Walt Disney*

We know not where our dreams will take us, but we can probably see quite clearly where we'll go without them.

◆ *Marilyn Grey*

Dreams come a size too big so that we can grow into them.

◆ *Josie Bisset*

If one is lucky, a solitary fantasy can totally transform one million realities.

◆ *Maya Angelou*

America is a nation always becoming, always defined by the great goals we set, the great dreams we dream. We are restless, questing people. We have always believed, with President Thomas Jefferson, that "freedom is the first born daughter of science." With that belief and with willpower, resources and great national effort, we have always reached our far horizons and set out for new ones.

◆ *Bill Clinton*

Go after your dream with a sense of entitlement. Know that you have the power to achieve it and that you deserve it. Be willing to get up into life's face, grab it by the collar and say, "Give it *up!* It's my dream."

Whatever you accomplish in life is a manifestation not so much of what you do, as of what you believe deeply within yourself that you deserve.

◆ *Les Brown*

I sincerely believe that there is a time in life for drifting. There is a time for sitting back and getting in touch with yourself. Some of our most interesting illuminations and ideas will come when we take time to reflect, time to kick back and cruise awhile.

But there's also a time for planning, a time for looking into the future, a time for more active participation in life. You can't cruise forever. The gas is running out, you're older and at a new stage of life. So I ask you, engage life actively! Embrace it and love it!

◆ *Rudolfo Anaya*

If you want a thing bad enough to go out and fight for it, to work day and night for it, to give up your time, your peace and your sleep for it ... if all that you dream and scheme is about it, and life seems useless and worthless without it ... if you gladly sweat for it and fret for it and plan for it and lose all your terror of the opposition for it ... if you simply go after that thing you want with all of your capacity, strength and sagacity, faith, hope and confidence and stern pertinacity ... if neither cold, poverty, famine, nor gout, sickness nor pain, of body and brain, can keep you away from the thing that you want ... if dogged and grim you beseech and beset it, with the help of God, you *will* get it.

◆ *Berton Bradley*

Until one is committed, there is hesitance, the chance to draw back. Always ineffectiveness. Concerning all acts of initiative (and creation), there is one elemental truth the ignorance of which kills countless ideas and splendid plans; that the moment one commits oneself, then providence moves too. All sorts of things occur to help one that would never have otherwise occurred. A whole stream of events issues from the decision, raising in one's favor all manner of unforeseen incidents and meetings and material assistance which no man could have dreamed would come his way. I have learned a deep respect for one of Goethe's couplets: "Whatever you can do, or dream you can, begin it. Boldness has genius, power and magic in it."

◆ *W. H. Murray*

To take a life, your life, and steer it in the direction you would like, toward the career you want and the fulfillment of your dreams, is the journey—the only real journey. No matter how rich or successful you think you are, unless you harness your dreams and continue to grow and develop, a boring, sedentary life will set in. Similarly, those who think they are at the bottom of the barrel, who feel apathetic and numb or think their lives have no chance—they, too, can turn it around and change. Whether you feel you're successful, at the bottom of the barrel, or somewhere in between, it's time to shake yourself into action and onto the road of your dreams.

◆ *Milton Katselas*

I will now give you your last lesson in metaphysics—nothing is as real as a dream. The world can change about you, but your dream will not. It will always be the link with the person you are today, young and full of hope. If you hold on to it you may grow old but you will never be old. And that, ladies and gentlemen, is the ultimate success.

◆ *Tom Clancy*

The older I get and the more I become aware that I have more yesterdays than tomorrows, the more I think that in our final hours, which all of us have to face, very rarely will we say, "Gosh, I wish I had spent more time at the office," or "If only I had made just a little more money." But we will think about the dreams we lived out, the wonders we knew, when we were most fully alive.

◆ *Bill Clinton*

It is your job to fulfill your Dream.

It is *not* your job to right all the wrongs of the world, to teach everyone everything you know so that *they* will be able to right all the wrongs of the world, to in any way become involved with the struggle that always has been and probably always will be part of this planet, or anything else.

Trust that that which is an area of your *concern*—but not of your Dream—*is* the Dream of others. Let them fulfill their Dream. You fulfill yours. "Nature arms each man with some faculty which enables him to do easily some feat impossible to any other," wrote Emerson. If we each bring our separate dish (our Dream) to the table of life—even if it's "just" dessert—we can all enjoy the banquet.

◆ *John-Roger & Peter McWilliams*

As you go out today to enter the clamorous highways of life, I should like to discuss with you some aspects of the American dream. For in a real sense, America is essentially a dream, a dream as yet unfulfilled. It is a dream of a land where men of all races, of all nationalities, and of all creeds can live together as brothers. The substance of that dream is expressed in these sublime words, words lifted to cosmic proportions: "We hold these truths to be self-evident, that all men are created equal, and that they are endowed by their Creator with certain inalienable rights; among these rights are life, liberty, and the pursuit of happiness." This is the dream.

◆ Martin Luther King, Jr.

Exercise the right to dream. You must face reality—that which is. But then dream of the reality that ought to be, that must be. Live beyond the pain of reality with the dream of a bright tomorrow. Use hope and imagination as a weapon of survival and progress. Use love to motivate you and obligate you to serve the human family.

◆ Jesse Jackson

All men and women are born, live, suffer and die; what distinguishes us one from another is our dreams, whether they be dreams about worldly or unworldly things, and what we do to make them come about. . . . We do not choose to be born. We do not choose our parents. We do not choose our historical epoch, the country of our birth, or the immediate circumstances of our upbringing. We do not, most of us, choose to die; nor do we choose the time and conditions of our death. But within this realm of choicelessness, we do choose how we live.

◆ Joseph Epstein

IF YOU THINK YOU CAN, YOU CAN!

You can be a total winner even if you're a beginner,
If you think you can, you can,
If you think you can, you can.
You can wear the gold medallion,
You can ride your own black stallion,
If you think you can, you can,
If you think you can, you can.

It's not your talent or the gift at birth,
It's not your bank book that determines worth,
And it isn't in the color of your skin,
It's your attitude that lets you win,
You can upset Connors or Austin,
Or win the marathon at Boston,
If you think you can, you can,
If you think you can, you can.

You can profit through inflation,
You can redirect this nation,
If you think you can, you can,
If you think you can, you can.

It doesn't matter if you've won before,
It makes no difference what's the halftime score,

It's never over until the final gun,
So keep on trying and you'll find you've won,
You grab your dream and then believe it,
Go out and work and you'll achieve it
If you think you can, you can!
If you think you can, you can!

Author unknown

The dreamers are the saviors of the world.

James Allen

CHILDHOOD DREAMS

I've spent my life wishing and dreaming of the future,
hoping it would come one day.
Weddings and love, a life unknown to me,
I'd lie in the sun thinking away.

But reality settles in and fades my dreams,
Life is far from those childhood wishes.

Now as my future comes
I wish for the past.
Times so simple and sweet.
A time when all I did was dream.

Rina Harbison

Be eager to dream.

Christopher Wren, who designed St. Paul's Cathedral in London, was one of the greatest of all English architects. One day, after work on his cathedral had begun, Wren walked unrecognized among the artisans and stonecutters. "What are you doing?" he asked one of the workmen. "I am cutting a piece of stone," the man replied. He put the same question to another. "I am earning five shillings twopence a day," the man said. He asked a third man the same question, and the man answered, "I am helping Sir Christopher Wren build a magnificent cathedral." That man had vision! He could see beyond the cutting of stone, beyond the earning of his daily wage, even beyond a single work of art—to the building of a magnificent cathedral.

You too must strive to attain your vision of the larger whole. If you do, no dream you will ever dream will be impossible to accomplish. Your dreams may be as magnificent as a great cathedral—the next great biological or technological discovery, or as modest as a perfectly cut piece of stone—being a good parent, a good spouse, a contributing member of your community, a caring advocate for the afflicted. The size of your dream is not important. What is important is that you allow yourself the opportunity. As the poet Douglas Malluch once wrote, "Success is not occupying a lofty place or doing conspicuous work, it is being the best that is in you . . . Do the things near at hand," he said, "and great things will come to your hands to be done."

President Reagan once spoke to a group of young astronauts about the importance of having a vision of the future and the courage to pursue it. Because I believe that you are every bit as much explorers on the brink of discovery as astronauts—perhaps even more so—I would like to paraphrase his advice for you. When you come to the edge of your known world, you will be standing on the shores of the infinite. Dip your hand in that limitless sea. Sail across its waters and embark on the boldest, most noble adventure of all. Out beyond your present horizons lie whole new continents of possibility, new worlds of hope waiting to be discovered. You have traveled far, but your journey has really only just begun. This is no time for small plans or shrinking ambitions. We stand on the threshold of an epic age—an age of technological splendor and an explosion of human potential.

Right now, you may feel inadequate to the challenges of the future—all graduates do. But you and those of your generation are better prepared to meet them than any generation that has gone before. America was founded by people with great courage who were not afraid to take great risks. People who greeted change—not with trepidation—but with energy and excitement and optimism.

Be prepared to adapt. Be willing to risk. Be eager to dream. If you are, your dreams will surely come true.

Bill Frist

THE DREAMS AHEAD

What would we do in this world of ours,
    Were it not for the dreams ahead?
For thorns are mixed with the blooming flowers,
    No matter which path we tread.

And each of us has his golden goal,
    Stretching far into the years;
And ever he climbs with a hopeful soul,
    With alternate smiles and tears.

That dream ahead is what holds him up
    Through the storms of a ceaseless fight;
When his lips are pressed to the wormwood's cup,
    And clouds shut out the light.

To some it's a dream of high estate
    To some it's a dream of wealth;
To some it's a dream of a truce with Fate
    In a constant search for health.

To some it's a dream of home and wife;
    To some it's a crown above;
The dreams ahead are what make each life—
    The dreams—and faith—and love!

       ◆ *Edwin Carlisle Litsey*

People at occasions like this often say something like—"Now we hope that you can realize your dreams." At the risk of sounding negative—I hope you don't realize all your dreams.

Do you know which are the most frequent dreams for Americans? The most common dream of all is that you're falling. Not failing, falling. Next is that you're being chased. Number 3 is that you're un-prepared for an exam—well, this one might not have been a dream but a reality for some of you.

The fourth most common dream is that you're standing naked in front of people—well, we don't need to worry about that tonight.

So you shouldn't try to realize all your dreams.

Steve Lodle

When your heart is in your dream, no request is too extreme. Are you disappointed, discouraged and discontented with your present level of success? Are you secretly dissatisfied with your present status? Do you want to become a better and more beautiful person than you are today? Would you like to be able to really learn how to be proud of yourself and still not lose genuine humility? Then start dreaming! It's possible! You can become the person you have always wanted to be!

Robert H. Schuller

Somehow I can't believe that there are any heights that can't be scaled by a man who knows the secrets of making dreams come true. This special secret, it seems to me, can be summarized in four C's. They are curiosity, confidence, courage, and constancy, and the greatest of all is confidence. When you believe in a thing, believe in it all the way, implicitly and unquestionably.

Walt Disney

Perhaps one of the reasons I have been asked to speak is that I turn fifty in a few weeks yet remain as excited about my future as I did thirty years ago when I was in college preparing to move on to a new phase in my life.

To me, life is a great adventure. A series of journeys within journeys, circles within circles. And like all great journeys, they begin with a dream. When I was growing up, dreams were, and still are, a major part of my life. Everyone should dream and then try to make those dreams come true. For me, my dreams dealt with adventure. My heroes were people like Marco Polo, Captain James Cook, and mythical characters out of Jules Verne's novels. One of my major heroes came from *Twenty Thousand Leagues Under the Sea,* with its nuclear submarine *Nautilus* and its great Captain Nemo. My biggest dream was to build a submarine myself and sail around the world underwater—to be Captain Nemo and look out of his magical window to see things no one had ever seen before.

I was lucky with my dreams. My father was an engineer and my older brother a physicist. To them the world was bound by the laws of physics. What a wonderful thing, the laws of physics. Wherever you go in the universe, they apply. If you were to travel to the far reaches of our galaxy and find a planet with intelligent life, those beings may have never heard of communism or capitalism or lawyers or politicians, but they would know the laws of physics. If God wrote any laws to govern us, He certainly wrote these laws. How could anyone be a great explorer like Captain Nemo and not know the laws ruling the planet?

This discovery was a lucky one for me. It meant that the dreams I had were governed by reality. I found that when I tried to live out my dreams, I could. If it obeyed the laws of physics, it was possible. And if it was possible, it was attainable, if I would only take the risk and try.

In an epic journey, after you have a dream, you begin to prepare yourself to pursue that dream. That is what many of you have been doing for the last four years. In my case, my journeys were physical journeys. That is what is so wonderful about what I do. I am able to leave society as we know it and travel to some distant place. Like Jason in search of the Golden Fleece or Ulysses on his odyssey.

When I was growing up, the landmasses of the world were largely explored—and the final frontiers were in space and underwater. Space fascinated me and still does, but the ocean fascinated me even more. I do not know if it was the pull of Nemo or that I grew up in San Diego and the sea was so much a part of my life, literally at my doorstep.

I can vividly remember walking among the beautiful sandy beaches of Southern California, searching for treasures washed ashore by the tide. I remember one day finding a Japanese fishing float which had traveled across the broad Pacific Ocean, a journey that must have taken years to complete, finally washing ashore, now waiting to be discovered. I can remember exploring the countless tidal pools at low tide, each a world unto itself. One might have a small school of fish racing around, trying to find a way out. Another an octopus hiding inside a tiny cave, hoping not to be seen. The ever-present sea anemones which closed when I touched them and the small crabs ready to stand their ground and fight to the death should I try to pick them up. I had a friend named Johnny Bickley who went with me on numerous adventures in San Diego Bay, watching the giant manta rays leap into the air, hooking onto a monster who effortlessly broke my line and swam away.

As I was growing up, the sea was always a part of my life. I graduated from walking along the beach and investigating tidal pools to bodysurfing and scuba diving. For some reason, I never had an interest in the top of the sea or, for that matter, the sea itself. It was the land beneath the sea that held my fascination. Perhaps it was my love of mountains. Every time I put on an air tank, I headed straight for the bottom. While in high school I wrote a letter to the Scripps Institution of Oceanography in La Jolla, a place I had visited many times before to see their aquarium or to fish on their pier, if I could sneak out onto it undetected. A kind scientist at Scripps answered my letter and told me how I could apply for a summer scholarship. I was seventeen years old and the summer of 1959 gave me my first great adventures with the sea. On the first cruise, we were hit by a great storm and limped back to shore. On the second, our ship was almost sunk by a great wave which knocked out the windows in the bridge and exploded the portholes in the galley. It was awesome to watch the waves crash over the ship. I was hooked.

On that cruise, I met another kind scientist who encouraged me to attend the University of California at Santa Barbara, where he was teaching geology. Not knowing exactly what aspect of the sea I wanted to concentrate on, I majored in all the physical sciences: physics, math, chemistry, and geology. It proved to be my most important decision. This broad-based education in science and technology has made it possible for me to follow the action in my field. I think it is a mistake to narrowly focus your interests. The broader your experience, the more you can go with the flow, as time goes on.

My childhood dreams always dealt with the sea. But before I could set out on a marine adventure, I had to prepare myself. To carry out my adventures required teamwork, leadership, discipline, and a knowledge about the sea, both technical and scientific.

For teamwork I turned to sports, which have always been an important part of my life—team sports like basketball to teach me to work with others and individual sports like tennis to teach me about myself.

Leadership and discipline came from the military, initially in the Army during the Vietnam era and later in the Navy, where I remain a commander in the Reserve. The military put me into major leadership positions long before I would have had that experience anywhere else.

Your childhood is spent dreaming, your young adulthood preparing. The moment finally comes when it is time to venture forth. If your dream is a big one you will need help, you will need to be part of a team. Initially, you will follow, but then you will lead. You will never make a good leader unless you have learned to follow. On those initial journeys when you are asked to pull your oar while another leads, learn what it takes to be a team player. Learn how to get along with others. Learn what loyalty and honesty are all about. Anyone can get to the top by taking shortcuts by climbing over the bodies of others, but if you take that route, your time at the top will be short-lived.

Finally, after working for years to help someone else live their dream, your turn will come. And when you lead your team on its first adventure in life, be prepared to fail initially. For no quest is worth pursuing that does not require you to pass many tests, take numerous risks. Jason had to tame the wild bulls, Ulysses had to resist the sirens calling him onto the rocks; Captain Nemo had to face the giant squid. Every major adventure I have been on over the years has tested me severely with violent storms and lost equipment. My first voyage to find the *Titanic* ended in failure. My first expedition to find the *Bismarck* failed as well. The test you must pass is not whether you fall down or not but whether you can get back up after being knocked down. The journeys you will now begin in life will test you to find how well you prepared your mind, but the hardest tests of all will look to see how determined you are to live your dream, how strong is your heart.

At times it will seem like the storms of life will never end, that the trials you must pass seem to go on forever, but they will end—only after your heart and mind have been tested. I have lived through countless storms at sea. Winds over one hundred miles an hour, swells reaching fifty feet. And when I thought I could not last another minute, the winds dropped off, the seas flattened, and the blue sky appeared and my quest was reached. Be it the *Titanic,* the *Bismarck,* or whatever goal I sought. For me, Neptune would finally say enough is enough. I had passed the test. The sea calmed and Neptune would pull back the veil of watery secrecy and there was what I had been looking for. There was the truth I sought.

Your journey is not over once your goal is reached, your dream fulfilled, the truth attained. The journey is never over until you share what you have learned with others. Then and only then can you begin preparing yourself for your next adventure. Sharing is the final step, when you give up what you have learned. Giving is not something that may interest you right now, but always remember life is never fulfilled, your journey never over until you take time to give back a portion of what has been given to you.

I congratulate all of you for dreaming dreams and preparing yourself to live those dreams. This is at hand to move on to the next phase. When life knocks you down, which it will, lay there for a second and reflect upon what has happened. Learn from your mistake but then get back up. Do not let anyone stop you from fulfilling your dreams.

◆   *Robert D. Ballard*

If you come to a thing with no preconceived notions of what that thing is, the whole world can be your canvas. Just dream it, and you can make it so. I believe I belong wherever I want to be, in whatever situation or context I place myself. . . .

So yeah, I think anything is possible. I know it because I have lived it. I know it because I have seen it. I have witnessed things the ancients would have called miracles, but they are not miracles. They are the products of someone's dream, and they happen as the result of hard work. Or they happen because, you know, shit happens. As human beings, we are capable of creating a paradise, and making each other's lives better by our own hands. Yes, yes, yes . . . this is possible.

Whoopi Goldberg

IT'S A LONG WAY

It's a long way the sea-winds blow
    Over the sea-plains blue, —
But longer far has my heart to go
    Before its dreams come true.

It's work we must, and love we must,
    And do the best we may,
And take the hope of dreams in trust
    To keep us day by day.

It's a long way the sea-winds blow —
    But somewhere lies a shore —

Thus down the tide of Time shall flow
　My dreams forevermore.

◆ *William Stanley Braithwaite*

That impossible dream you dreamed when you were young but got talked out of, the one you thought you outgrew, might be the key to awakening your genius. That special talent you never followed through on might be an important source of delight, the one you should commit to. That old dream might be the one thing that will bring the magic of meaning to your life.

◆ *Mark Victor Hansen &*
Barbara Nichols

HOLD FAST YOUR DREAMS

Hold fast your dreams!
Within your heart
Keep one still, secret spot
Where dreams may go,
And, sheltered so,
May thrive and grow
Where doubt and fear are not.
Oh keep a place apart,
Within your heart,
For little dreams to go!

Think still of lovely things that are not true.
Let wish and magic work at will in you.
Be sometimes blind to sorrow. Make believe!
Forget the calm that lies
In disillusioned eyes.
Though we all know that we must die,
Yet you and I
May walk like gods and be
Even now at home in immortality.

We see so many ugly things—
Deceits and wrongs and quarrelings;
We know, Alas! we know
How quickly fade
The color in the west,
The bloom upon the flower,
The bloom upon the breast
And youth's blind hour.
Yet keep within your heart
A place apart
Where little dreams may go,
May thrive and grow.
Hold fast—hold fast your dreams!

Louise Driscoll

The one common link among all unstoppable people is adversity—they struggled, tripped and stumbled, and had setbacks and failures, but they pulled themselves up and kept on going. The dream demanded their all and they gave it. The challenges and hardships they faced seemed insurmountable and yet they surmounted them. With each trial, they emerged stronger, surer, and more deserving of the dream itself.

◆ *Cynthia Kersey*

YOU CAN GO AS FAR AS YOUR DREAMS CAN TAKE YOU

If you can reach out, you can hold on.
If you can imagine, you can achieve.
If you just begin, you can continue.
Search within, and you'll find a reason to believe.

If you can get involved, you can make it happen.
If you can give, you will be rewarded with the taking.
If you can climb, you can climb even higher.
Envision it; your success is in the making.

If you trust the winner within you, you will win.
If you can keep your courage, you will go so far.
If you follow your ambitions, your course will guide you
towards a ladder that you can climb to your stars.

If you don't put limits on yourself,
you can always keep striving.
You might amaze yourself with what
you discover you can do.
If you want to reach out for happiness,
don't ever forget these words:

You can go as far as your dreams can take you.

◆ *Colin McCarty*

Ask yourself: What would be a great thing to do with my life before I die? Whatever it is, decide to do it! If it's more education you need, get it! If it's more money you need, find it! Whatever you do—don't blow the opportunities that are still before you. God is desperately trying to instill a dream into your imagination. Don't torpedo it by saying it's impossible.

◆ *Robert H. Schuller*

Believe in what makes you feel good.
Believe in what makes you happy.
Believe in the dreams
    you've always wanted to come true,
    and give them every chance to.

Life holds no promises
    as to what will come your way.

You must search towards reaching them.
Life makes no guarantees
    as to what you'll have.
It just gives you time to make choices
    and to take chances
and to discover whatever secrets
    might come your way.

If you are willing to take
    the opportunities you are given
    and utilize the abilities you have,
you will constantly fill your life
    with special moments
    and unforgettable times.

No one knows the mysteries of life
    or its ultimate meaning,
but for those who are willing
    to believe in their dreams,
    and in themselves,
life is a precious gift,
    in which anything is possible.

                        ◆ *Dena Dilaconi*

I want to talk about the activity you are always warned against as being wasteful, impractical, hopeless. I want to talk about dreaming. . . . We are in a mess, you know, and we have to get out. . . .

Well, now, you may be asking yourself, "What is all of this? I can't save the world. What about my life? I didn't come here for this. I didn't even ask to come here. I didn't ask to be born." Didn't you? I put it to you that you did. You not only asked to be born, you insisted on your life. That's why you're here. There's no other reason. It's too easy not to have been born, and now that you're here, you have to do something. Something you respect, don't you? Your parents may have wanted you, but they did not dream you up. You did that. I'm just urging you to continue the dream you started, because dreaming is not irresponsible. It's first order, human business. It's not entertainment, you know. It's work. When Martin Luther King said, "I have a dream," he wasn't playing; he was serious. When he imagined it, envisioned, created it in his own mind, it began. Now we have to dream it too and give it the heft and stretch and longevity it deserves, but don't let anybody convince you this is the way the world is and therefore must be. It must be the way it ought to be. . . .

You are not helpless and you're not heartless, and you have time. Thank you.

> *Toni Morrison*

A teenage girl on the verge of high school graduation sits in a fairly empty boardroom, as nine men and women debate the costs of renovating the downtown area of the small farming community in which she lives. As their voices drone on in the background, her mind wanders. She notices various things around her, all of them odd, of course. The fuzzballs on her black-and-white checkered socks, the spot on her jeans from a run-in with something dirty at work earlier in the day, and the city seal on the wall in front of her. In a frantic attempt to find more things to divert her attention, she notices the empty chair to her left. As she turns her head, she hopes to see a smiling face with bright blue eyes looking back at her. Maybe he is making her a word search, writing a note, waiting for their next thumb-wrestling match, or doing anything else to avoid paying attention to the debate, which is much less than interesting. At any rate, he is there, and together they make the dull moments much more interesting. As she pictures this to herself, a smile appears on her face and, in the middle of a very serious moment, she wants to laugh.

And laugh she does. The room falls silent, all eyes focusing on the source of the noise. A council member suddenly rises to his feet. "My dear, if you find these matters light of heart, please feel free to leave."

Quickly snapping out of her trance, she stammers, "Actually, sir, there is nothing more I'd rather do. Oh, and by the way, that suit is ugly and your wig is slanted a tad bit to the left. You have a nice night." Grabbing her belongings and quickly rising to her feet, she makes her way out of the city chambers. Pushing her way through the glass double doors, she meets the cool air of the night. Reaching for a pen she had stolen from the bank earlier in the day, she fixes her soft brown hair into a bun on the back of her head. Although unusually cool for early May, the night air on her warm neck is refreshing to her. Opting to leave the car where it is, she turns up the street. Within minutes, she finds herself walking along a rural road. Leaving the sidewalk to lay in the tall grass of a field, she gazes at the clear stars above. She begins to think deeply, as she is prone to do, wondering what exactly those stars hold for her. Where will her future take her? What will it bring?

She takes her hair out of the bun and begins to play with it. As she lies there in the grass below the beautiful stars, smiling to herself, she feels a tear roll down her cheek. She is sad all of a sudden, feeling alone and incredibly frightened. The very distant future she has been dreaming about for so many years is not so distant anymore. . . .

◆　*Kelly Leddy*

Reaching for the Stars

◆ ◆ ◆

People are always blaming their circumstances for what they are. I don't believe in circumstances. The people who get on in this world are the people who get up and look for the circumstances they want, and, if they can't find them, they make them.

◆ *George Bernard Shaw*

May you build a ladder to the stars
And climb on every rung,
May you stay forever young.

◆ *Bob Dylan*

Risk the fall in order to fly.

◆ *Karen Goldman*

I always have to dream up there against the stars. If I don't dream I will make it, I won't even get close.

◆ *Henry J. Kaiser*

Only from the heart
Can you touch the sky.

◆ *Rumi*

Reality is something you rise above.

◆ *Liza Minnelli*

[When I was a kid] I needed structure and attention. I require a lot of attention. And now I get the attention of 20 million people. That's a little too much attention. I wanted it, I got it.

◆ *Oprah Winfrey*

We know what we are, but not what we may be.

◆ *William Shakespeare*

I thought I had to make an impact on history. It was quite simple. I had to become the greatest choreographer of my time. That was my mission, and that's what I set out to do.

◆ *Twyla Tharp*

There is nothing standing in your way to do whatever you want to do provided you know what you want to do and love to do it. Education is no value, talent is worthless, unless you have one unwavering aim. Never find yourself without a compass.

◆ *Condoleezza Rice*

Only passions, great passions, can elevate the soul to great things.

Denis Diderot

The starting point of all achievement is desire. Keep this constantly in mind. Weak desires bring weak results, just as a small amount of fire makes a small amount of heat.

Napoleon Hill

The most powerful weapon on earth is the human soul on fire.

Marshal Ferdinand Foch

If you look at any of the most successful people in history, you will find this common thread: They would not be denied. They would not accept no. They would not allow anything to stop them from making their vision, their goal, a reality. Did you know that Walt Disney was turned down 302 times before he got financing for his dream of creating "The Happiest Place on Earth"? All the banks thought he was crazy.

He wasn't crazy; he was a visionary and, more important, he was committed to making that vision a reality. Today, millions of people have shared in "the joy of Disney," a world like no other, a world launched by the decision of one man.

◆ *Anthony Robbins*

If you want to achieve great things in your life, you have to take risks. The first risk is daring to feel deeply, to be passionate about what you want and care about. Enthusiasm is the key to breaking through barriers, whether your dream is to touch one person or millions.

◆ *Ken Kragen*

I tell you the truth, if you have faith as small as a mustard seed, you can say to this mountain, "Move from here to there," and it will move. Nothing will be impossible for you.

◆ *Matthew 17:20*

Again and again, first prizes don't go to the most talented man—again and again the man who wins is the one who is sure that he can! A powerful fact is this: *A great drive, a powerful determination, a consuming desire, will easily compensate for little or limited talent.*

◆ *Robert H. Schuller*

You have to set the goals that are almost out of reach. If you set a goal that is attainable without much work or thought, you are stuck with something below your true talent and potential.

◆ *Steve Garvey*

We need to learn to set our course by the stars, not by the lights of every passing ship.

Gen. Omar Nelson Bradley

Keep your feet on the ground and keep reaching for the stars.

Casey Kasem

If you're climbing the ladder of life, you go rung by rung, one step at a time. Don't look too far up, set your goals high but take one step at a time. Sometimes you don't think you're progressing until you step back and see how high you've really gone.

Donny Osmond

It's the moment you think you can't that you realize you can.

Celine Dion

Reach up as far as you can, and God will reach down all the way.

Author unknown

If you don't fail now and again, it's a sign you're playing it safe.

Woody Allen

Reach high, for stars lie hidden in your soul. Dream deep, for every dream precedes the goal.

Pamela Vaull Starr

The human spirit is so great a thing that no man can express it; could we rightly comprehend the mind of man nothing would be impossible to us upon the earth.

◆ *Paracelsus*

The One who is full of grace
Will find the ladder to the sky.

◆ *Rumi*

I want to put a ding in the universe.

◆ *Steve Jobs* (CEO, Apple)

There are glimpses of heaven to us in every act, or thought, or word, that raises us above ourselves.

◆ *Arthur P. Stanley*

Keep your feet on the ground, but let your heart soar as high as it will. Refuse to be average or to surrender to the chill of your spiritual environment.

◆ *A. W. Tozer*

We've removed the ceiling above our dreams. There are no more impossible dreams.

◆ *Jesse Jackson*

If you have built castles in the air, your work need not be lost; that is where they should be. Now put the foundations under them.

◆ *Henry David Thoreau*

Do or not do. There is no try.

◆ *Yoda*

If you want a place in the sun, you must leave the shade of the family tree.

◆ *Osage saying*

Everything I did in my life that was worthwhile I caught hell for.

◆ *Earl Warren*

Do not be too timid and squeamish about your actions. All life is an experiment.

◆ *Ralph Waldo Emerson*

What is man anyway? Man is flesh and blood, body and mind, bones and muscle, arms and legs, heart and soul, lungs and liver, nerves and veins—all these and more make a man. But man is really what his dreams are. Man is what he aspires to be. He is the ideals that beckon him on. Man is the integrity that keeps him steadfast, honest, and true. If a young man tells me what he aspires to be, I can almost predict his future.

An individual cannot aspire if he or she looks down. The Creator has not molded us with aspirations and longings for heights to which we cannot climb. Look upward. The unattained calls us to climb new mountains. You cannot have too much of that emotion called ambition, for, even though you do not attain your idea, the efforts you make will bring nothing but blessings. Life should be lived in earnest; it is no idle game, no farce to amuse and be forgotten.

Benjamin E. Mays

Never measure the height of a mountain, until you have reached the top. Then you will see how low it was.

Dag Hammarskjöld

When you reach for the stars, you may not quite get one, but you won't come up with a handful of mud, either.

Leo Burnett

The only way to discover the limits of the possible is to go beyond them into the impossible.

Arthur C. Clarke

There are two things to aim at in life: first, to get what you want and, after that, to enjoy it. Only the wisest of mankind achieve the second.

Logan Pearsall Smith

Don't bunt. Aim out of the ball park. Aim for the company of the immortals.

David Ogilvy

Trust yourself. Create the kind of self that you will be happy to live with all your life. Make the most of yourself by fanning the tiny, inner sparks of possibility into flames of achievement.

Foster C. Mcclellan

All life is a chance. So take it! The person who goes furthest is the one who is willing to do and dare.

Dale Carnegie

Be bold, and mighty forces will come to your aid.

Basil King

If I were to wish for anything, I should not wish for wealth and power, but for the passionate sense of the potential, for the eye which, ever young and ardent, sees the possible. Pleasure disappoints, possibility never. And what wine is so sparkling, what so fragrant, what so intoxicating, as possibility!

Søren Kierkegaard

In the long run you hit only what you aim at. Therefore, though you should fail immediately, you had better aim at something high.

Henry David Thoreau

Mama exhorted her children at every opportunity to "jump at de sun." We might not land on the sun, but at least we would get off the ground.

Zora Neale Hurston

To laugh is to risk appearing the fool.

To weep is to risk appearing sentimental.

To reach for another is to risk involvement.

To expose your ideas, your dreams, before a crowd, is to risk their loss.

To love is to risk not being loved in return.

To live is to risk dying.

To believe is to risk failure.

But risks must be taken, because the greatest hazard in life is to risk nothing.

The people who risk nothing do nothing, have nothing, are nothing.

They may avoid suffering and sorrow, but they cannot learn, feel, change, grow, love, live.

Chained by their attitudes, they are slaves; they have forfeited their freedom.

Only a person who risks is free.

Anonymous

Life is meant to be fun, and fun is a sure antidote to disappointment. A million things have brought me joy, or laughter, or most important, the experience of beauty. Read. Plant a potato, and discover a treasure chest of new ones when you dig them. Walk down a northern path in springtime, and try to count the dogwood blossoms and the trilliums. Read Shakespeare. Discover love. Then look up at the stars and reach for them.

Richard Cutler

One can never consent to creep when one feels an impulse to soar.

◆ *Helen Keller*

The young do not know enough to be prudent, and therefore they attempt the impossible—and achieve it, generation after generation.

◆ *Pearl S. Buck*

We know how rough the road will be, how heavy here the load will be, we know about the barricades that wait along the track, but we have set our soul upon a certain goal ahead and nothing left from hell to sky shall ever turn us back.

◆ *Vince Lombardi*

Become a possibilitarian. No matter how dark things seem to be or actually are, raise your sights and see possibilities—always see them, for they're always there.

◆ *Norman Vincent Peale*

Everything is possible for him who believes.

◆ *Mark 9:23*

We all have possibilities we don't know about. We can do things we don't even dream we can do.

◆ *Dale Carnegie*

A lot of successful people are risk-takers. Unless you're willing to do that, to have a go, to fail miserably, and have another go, success won't happen.

◆ *Phillip Adams*

You can't expect to hit the jackpot if you don't put a few nickels in the machine.

◆ *Flip Wilson*

Our greatest glory is not in never falling, but in rising every time we fall.

◆ *Confucius*

To climb steep hills requires slow pace at first.

◆ *William Shakespeare*

You have everything but one thing—madness. A man needs a little madness or else—he never dares cut the rope and be free.

◆ *Zorba the Greek*

If you aren't going all the way, why go at all?

◆ *Joe Namath*

Every man has the right to risk his own life in order to save it.

◆ *Jean-Jacques Rousseau*

When in doubt, make a fool of yourself. There is a microscopically thin line between being brilliantly creative and acting like the most gigantic idiot on earth. So what the hell, leap.

> ◆ *Cynthia Meimel*

I always thought I should be treated like a star.

> ◆ *Madonna*

Never bend your head. Hold it high. Look the world straight in the eye.

> ◆ *Helen Keller*

Even when I went to the playground, I never picked the best players. I picked the guys with less talent, but who were willing to work hard . . . and put in the effort, who had the desire to be great.

> ◆ *Earvin "Magic" Johnson*

Whether or not you reach your goals in life depends entirely on how well you prepare for them and how badly you want them.

> ◆ *Ronald McNair*

We can do whatever we wish to do provided our wish is strong enough.

> ◆ *Katherine Mansfield*

The fireworks begin today. Each diploma is a lighted match. Each one of you is a fuse.

> ◆ *Ed Koch*

You have to expect things of yourself before you can do them.

Michael Jordan

I believe we can fly on the wings we create.

Melissa Etheridge

Aim at the sun, and you may not reach it; but your arrow will fly far higher than if aimed at an object on a level with yourself.

J. Hawes

Man's reach should exceed his grasp, or what's a heaven for?

Robert Browning

Never give in! Never give in! Never, never, never, never. . . . In nothing great or small, large or petty, never give in except to convictions or honor and good sense!

Sir Winston Churchill

YOUR DIMENSION OF GREATNESS

No one can know the potential,
Of a life that is committed to win;
With courage—the challenge it faces,
To achieve great success in the end!

So, explore the Dimension of Greatness,
And believe that the world *can* be won;

By a mind that is fully committed,
Knowing the task can be done!

Your world has no place for the skeptic,
No room for the *doubter* to stand;
To weaken your firm resolution
That you *can excel* in this land!

We must have *vision to see* our potential,
And *faith to believe* that we can;
Then *courage to act* with conviction,
To become what *God meant* us to be!

So, possess the strength and the courage,
To conquer *whatever* you choose;
It's the person *who never gets started,*
That is destined *forever* to lose!

◆   *Author unknown*

Shoot for the moon. Even if you miss it, you will land among the stars.

◆   *Les Brown*

Far away in the sunshine are my highest inspirations. I may not reach them, but I can look up and see the beauty, believe in them and try to follow where they lead.

◆   *Louisa May Alcott*

I realized that if I was going to achieve anything in life I had to be aggressive. I had to get out there and go for it. I don't believe you can achieve anything by being passive. I'm not thinking about anything except what I'm trying to accomplish. Any fear is an illusion. You think something is standing in your way, but nothing is really there. What is there is an opportunity to do your best and gain some success. If it turns out my best isn't good enough, then at least I'll never be able to look back and say I was too afraid to try. Failure always made me try harder the next time. Obstacles don't have to stop you. If you run into a wall, don't turn around and give up. Figure out how to climb it, go through it, or work around it.

Michael Jordan

He turns not back who is bound to a star.

Leonardo da Vinci

From a little spark may burst a mighty flame.

Dante Alighieri

If you want a place in the sun, you've got to put up with a few blisters.

Abigail Van Buren

Even a small star shines in the darkness.

Finnish proverb

We are all in the gutter, but some of us are looking at the stars.

Oscar Wilde

I think that's precisely what growing up is—steadily learning to take more and greater risks. While it's easy—and helpful—to see this facility for risk-taking growing in a child, it's important to remember that this process continues all our lives.

◆ *Gloria Steinem*

Do it big or stay in bed.

◆ *Larry Kelly*

Enthusiasm is the most important thing in life.

◆ *Tennessee Williams*

If you surrender to the wind, you can ride it.

◆ *Toni Morrison*

There is in this world no such force as the force of a man determined to rise.

◆ *W. E. B. Du Bois*

Maurice Sendak, author of *Where the Wild Things Are*, once recounted that he sent to a young reader a card with a picture of a Wild Thing on it, and the boy's mother wrote back that her son loved the card so much he ate it. He didn't seem to care that it was an original Maurice Sendak drawing. He just saw it, he loved it, he ate it.

Passion is a state of love, and hunger. It is also a state of enthusiasm, which means to be possessed by a god or a goddess, by a Wild

Thing. One could be possessed by the god of poetry or the goddess of animals, the god of commerce or the goddess of home and hearth. If we imagine that calls issue from the gods, then we are as close as we ever get to them—the calls *and* the gods—when we are enthusiastic. We move toward a kind of divine *presence* because, through our passions, we are utterly present. We are utterly charged and focused. We are oblivious, we forget ourselves, our troubles, our day-to-day living-on-Mulberry-Street lives. We hitch ourselves to something bigger.

◆ *Gregg Levoy*

No matter how far a person can go the horizon is still way beyond you.

◆ *Zora Neale Hurston*

He who is not courageous enough to take risks will accomplish nothing in life.

◆ *Muhammad Ali*

Life is like a ten-speed bike. Most of us have gears we never use.

◆ *Charles M. Schulz*

There is a giant asleep within every man.
When the giant awakes, miracles happen.

◆ *Frederick Faust*

Each person on this planet is inherently, intrinsically capable of attaining "dizzying heights" of happiness and fulfillment. The main barrier to most people's doing so seems to be fear, fear that the heights will make them dizzy instead of rooting their feet more firmly to the ground, which is what actually happens. . . .

There seems to be a widespread fear in our society of flying too close to the sun, of gaining too much and consequently losing it; of getting too happy and falling down. . . . "The sky's the limit" may be a cliché . . . but the oldest clichés and stock phrases in our language usually contain the most truth, if we see them in their proper contexts; and if we really think about it, "The sky's the limit" turns out to be *most true* when applied to the potentials of human beings. . . .

So the next time you look at the sky in bewilderment and wonder, remember, you have within you far greater mysteries than this.

◆ *Wayne Dyer*

You've got to dance like there's nobody watching. You've got to love like you'll never get hurt. You've got to come from the heart if you want it to work.

◆ *Susanna Clarke*

Far better is it to dare mighty things, to win glorious triumphs, even though checkered with failure, than to take rank with those poor spirits who neither enjoy much nor suffer much, because they live in that gray twilight that knows not victory nor defeat.

◆ *Theodore Roosevelt*

Our aspirations are our possibilities.

◆ *Robert Browning*

Everyone has inside of him a piece of good news. The good news is that you don't know how great you can be! How much you can love! What you can accomplish! And what your potential is!

◆ *Anne Frank*

Whatever the mind of man can *conceive* and *believe* it can *achieve.*

◆ *Napoleon Hill*

Altitude is determined by attitude . . . high achievers shoot for the stars; if they fall short of their mark, at least they come back with stardust in their hands.

◆ *Dennis Kimbro*

Set your goals high, and don't stop till you get there.

◆ *Bo Jackson*

Make no little plans: they have no magic to stir men's blood . . . make big plans, aim high in hope and work.

◆ *Daniel H. Burnham*

Twenty years from now you will be more disappointed by the things you didn't do than by the ones you did do. So throw off the bowlines. Sail away from the safe harbor. Catch the trade winds in your sails. Explore. Dream. Discover.

◆ *Author unknown*

Don't let the fear of striking out hold you back.

Babe Ruth

Only those who dare to fail greatly can ever achieve greatly.

Robert F. Kennedy

© 1977 Jim Unger/dist. by LaughingStock Licensing Inc.

**"Listen, there's nothing wrong
with being ambitious."**

I always want to do the best that I can with the opportunities that God has given me. The only way that you can do that is to give yourself the chance to go as high as you possibly can. If you don't have the confidence in yourself and you don't have the desire to compete and move ahead, then you start to get stagnant. . . . If I fall a little bit short, then I'm still further ahead than if I hadn't reached at all.

◆ *Don Shula*

Go out on the limb—that's where the fruit is.

◆ *Will Rogers*

You have powers you never dreamed of. You can do things you never thought you could do. There are no limitations in what you can do except the limitations of your own mind.

◆ *Darwin P. Kingsley*

There is one last bit of advice I would like to leave you with, and for this we move into more sobering territory. In an effort to find a phrase or a word that I would like to pass on as inspirational, I thought about what best expressed the theme of my own life. It is a word I mentioned just a few moments before: passion! It is the force that has governed and motivated all my energies, that has given me the discipline that is mandatory in all creative efforts and that without it, life seems to me rather bleak and dismal.

In the play *Amadeus,* Salieri, the court composer, realizing young

Mozart's genius when he hears his music for the first time, contemplates his own mediocre gifts by comparison and confides to the audience, "Is it enough just to have passion?" My daughter Nancy, who saw the play and was quite affected by it, talked to me about her own aspirations and, questioning her own abilities and talents, asked me the very same question. "Is it enough just to have passion?" My answer was, "It is not only enough. It is everything." I have seen more talented and gifted people fail to attain their aspirations because of a lack of passion, which I can only describe as a flame that burns within us with such intense heat that it glows with a pure white light and cannot be extinguished by despair, misfortune, infirmity, or not being at home when an important phone call comes in. Passion is the Super Bowl of enthusiasm. To have a passion for life is not only to wake up in the morning and hear birds singing, but it is taking the time to open the window to see where they are perched on the tree. That is one of the side benefits of passion. You pay attention to details. And it is the details that determine the quality of life. . . .

More simply stated, whatever path you follow from the moment you hopefully take off those long black gowns, do it as though Gershwin had written music to underscore your every move. Romantic and idealistic, yes. But I cannot think of anything in life worthwhile that was achieved without a great desire to achieve it. . . .

There is, to be fair, the flip side of passion. It is caution and timidity caused by an acute fear of failure. I can tell you from my own experience that the fear of failure is infinitely greater than failure. Waiting with bated breath to hear the reviews on an opening night is torture.

To finally hear the reviews, if they are favorable, is both joyous and unexpected. If they are negative, they are despairing and surprising. Surprising because although you may be despairing, you are also alive, breathing normally, drinking some Perrier and, with a little help from your friends, eating some pasta and a little chocolate mousse. In my own case, failure gets me up earlier the next morning than success. If you get right back to work, yesterday's pain becomes today's inspiration. . . .

Do not listen to those who say, "It is not done that way." Maybe it is not, but maybe you will. Do not listen to those who say, "You're taking too big a chance." If he did not take a big chance, Michelangelo would have painted the Sistine floor and it would surely be rubbed out today. Most importantly, do not listen to yourself when the little voice of fear inside of you rears its ugly head and says, "They are all smarter than you out there. They are more talented, they are taller, blonder, prettier, luckier, and have connections. They have a cousin who took out Meryl Streep's baby-sitter." Give any credence at all to that voice, and your worst fears will surely come true. Do not turn over power so easily. Do not make those who speak with a louder voice automatically right. Respect is one thing, submission another. Walk into any situation in life—whether it is professional, artistic, competitive, or personal—with a lack of self-esteem and you have just turned over the upper hand to someone who may not have even asked for it. I firmly believe that if you follow a path that interests you—hopefully with a passion—and if you bring to it a sense of your own worth—not to the exclusion of love, sensitivity, and cooperation with others, but with the strength of conviction that you can move others by your own efforts—and do not make success or failure the criteria by which you live, the chances are you will be a person worthy of your own respect.

◆ *Neil Simon*

If we did all the things we are capable of doing, we would literally astonish ourselves.

◆ *Thomas A. Edison*

As a human being, there are anchors tied to my feet, but I don't care, I fly anyway.

◆ *Karen Goldman*

Blessings on your young courage, boy; that's the way to the stars.

◆ *Virgil*

Big shots are only little shots who keep shooting.

◆ *Christopher Morley*

It is impossible to win the great prizes of life without running risks.

◆ *Theodore Roosevelt*

Risk more than others think is safe. Care more than others think is wise. Dream more than others think is practical. Expect more than others think is possible.

◆ *Cadet maxim*

It must be borne in mind that the tragedy of life does not lie in not reaching your goals, the tragedy lies in not having any goals to reach. It isn't a calamity to die with dreams unfulfilled, but it is a calamity not to dream. It is not a disaster to be unable to capture your ideals, but it is a disaster to have no ideals to capture. It is not a disgrace not to reach the stars, but it is a disgrace to have no stars to reach.

Benjamin E. Mays

Of course we all have our limits, but how can you possibly find your boundaries unless you explore as far and as wide as you possibly can? I would rather fail in an attempt at something new and uncharted than safely succeed in a repeat of something I have done.

A. E. Hotchner

How far is far, how high is high?
We'll never know until we try.

Song from the California Special Olympics

If your ship doesn't come in, swim out to it.

Jonathan Winters

Only those who will risk going too far can possibly find out how far one can go.

T. S. Eliot

It is not the critic who counts. Not the one who points out how the strong man stumbled or the doer of deeds might have done them better. The credit belongs to the man who is actually in the arena, whose face is marred with sweat and dust and blood. Who strives valiantly, who errs and comes short again and again. Who knows the great enthusiasms, the great devotions and spends himself in a worthy cause. Who, if he wins, knows the triumph of high achievement, and who, if he fails, at least does so while daring greatly so that his place shall never be with those cold and timid souls who know neither victory or defeat.

◆ *Theodore Roosevelt*

Living at risk is jumping off the cliff and building your wings on the way down.

◆ *Ray Bradbury*

Take a chance! All life is a chance. The man who goes the furthest is generally the one who is willing to do and dare. The "sure thing" boat never gets far from shore.

◆ *Dale Carnegie*

"How does one become a butterfly?" she asked pensively. "You must want to fly so much that you are willing to give up being a caterpillar."

◆ *Trina Paulus*

No one can really pull you up very high—you lose your grip on the rope. But on your own two feet you can climb mountains.

◆ *Louis Brandeis*

Are you in earnest? Seize this very minute;
Whatever you can do, or dream you can, begin it!
Boldness has genius, power and magic in it.
Only engage, and then the mind grows heated;
Begin, and then the work will be completed.

◆ *Johann Wolfgang von Goethe*

The advice I have to give you is, do not live your life safely. I would take risks and not do things just because everybody else does them. In my generation someone who had a big impact on me was Robert Kennedy, who in one speech said, "Some people see things the way they are and ask why, and others dream things that never were and ask why not?" I think that is where I hope many of you will be—people that question why things are and why we have to do them the way we have always done them. I hope you will take some risks, exert some real leadership on issues, and if you will, dance along the edge of the roof as you continue your life here.

◆ *Wilma Mankiller*

In great attempts it is glorious even to fail.

◆ *Vince Lombardi*

In the name of the best within you, do not sacrifice this world to those who are at its worst. In the name of the values that keep you alive, do not let your vision of man be distorted by the ugly, the cowardly, the mindless in those who have never achieved his title. Do not lose your knowledge that man's proper estate is an upright posture, an intransigent mind and a step that travels unlimited roads. Do not let your fire go out, spark by irreplaceable spark, in the hopeless swamps of the approximate, the not-quite, the not-yet, the not-at-all. Do not let the hero in your soul perish, in lonely frustration for the life you deserved, but have never been able to reach. Check your road and the nature of your battle. The world you desired can be won, it exists, it is real, it's yours.

◆ *Ayn Rand*

"Come to the edge," he said.
They said, "We are afraid."
"Come to the edge," he said.
They came.
He pushed them. . .
And they flew.

◆ *Guillaume Apollinaire*

Just do it.

◆ *Nike ad*

Think big. Big things happen to big-thinking people. Nothing big happens to little-thinking people.

You can become the person you want to be. It's possible. You'll discover this as you begin to break free from the tiger cage of impossibility thinking.

Join in a grand adventure of discovering the beautiful life God has been planning for you. Join the exciting crowd of energetic, enthusiastic, youthful possibility thinkers.

♦ *Robert H. Schuller*

GRADATIM

Heaven is not reached at a single bound,
　　But we build the ladder by which we rise
　　From the lowly earth to the vaulted skies,
And we mount to its summit round by round.

I count this thing to be grandly true:
　　That a noble deed is a step toward God—
　　Lifting the soul from the common clod
To a purer air and a broader view.

We rise by the things that are under our feet;
　　By what we have mastered of good and gain;
　　By the pride deposed and the passion slain,
And the vanquished ills that we hourly meet.

We hope, we aspire, we resolve, we trust,
　　When the morning calls us to life and light,
　　But our hearts grow weary, and, ere the night
Our lives are trailing the sordid dust.

We hope, we resolve, we aspire, we pray,
  And we think that we mount the air on wings
  Beyond the recall of sensual things,
While our feet still cling to the heavy clay.

Wings for the angels, but feet for men—
  We may borrow the wings to find the way—
  We may hope, and resolve, and aspire and pray,
But our feet must rise, or we fall again.

Only in dreams is a ladder thrown
  From the weary earth to the sapphire walls;
  But the dreams depart, and the vision falls,
And the sleeper wakes on his pillow of stone.

Heaven is not reached at a single bound,
  But we build the ladder by which we rise
  From the lowly earth to the vaulted skies,
And we mount to its summit round by round.

◆ *J. G. Holland*

Aim for your star, no matter how far, you must reach high above
and touch your life with love, you must never look back, but charge on!
Attack! See your goal, your star of desire, see it red hot, feel it burning,
you must be obsessed with it to make it your true yearning, be ready

my friends for when you truly believe it, you will certainly achieve it and by all of God's universal laws you will always receive it!

◆ *Bob Smith*

In playing ball, or in life, a person occasionally gets the opportunity to do something great. When that time comes, only two things matter: being prepared to seize the moment and having the courage to take your best swing.

◆ *Hank Aaron*

Every memorable act in the history of the world is a triumph of enthusiasm. Nothing great was ever achieved without it because it gives any challenge or any occupation, no matter how frightening or difficult, a new meaning. Without enthusiasm you are doomed to a life of mediocrity but with it you can accomplish miracles.

◆ *Og Mandino*

From undiscovered regions
Only the angels know,
Great winds of aspiration
Perpetually blow.

◆ *Bliss Carman*

I was taught that everything is attainable if you are prepared to give up, to sacrifice, to get it. Whatever you want to do, you can do it, if you want it badly enough, and I do believe that. I believe that if I wanted to run a mile in four minutes I could do it. I would have to give up everything else in my life, but I could run a mile in four minutes. I believe that if a man wanted to walk on water and was prepared to give up everything else in life, he could do that.

◆ *Stirling Moss*

Progress always involves risks. You can't steal second base and keep your foot on first.

◆ *Frederick B. Wilcox*

Down how many roads among the stars must man propel himself in search of the final secret? The journey is difficult, immense, at times impossible, yet that will not deter some of us from attempting it. . . . We have joined the caravan, you might say, at a certain point; we will travel as far as we can, but we cannot in one lifetime see all that we would like to see or learn all that we hunger to know.

◆ *Loren Eiseley*

And the world will be better for this
That one man scorned and covered with scars
Still strove with his last ounce of courage
To reach the unreachable star.

◆ *Joe Darion*

Get out of that slow lane. Shift into the fast lane. If you think you can't, you won't. If you think you can, there's a good chance you will.

Even making the effort will make you feel like a new person. Reputations are made by searching for things that can't be done and doing them. Aim low: boring. Aim high: soaring.

◆ *Richard Kerr*

I am the greatest.
I said that even before I knew I was.
Don't tell me I can't do something.
Don't tell me it's impossible.
Don't tell me I'm not the greatest.
I'm the double greatest.

◆ *Muhammad Ali*

Too many people today are afraid to step up to bat. They are afraid that life is going to throw them all kinds of curve balls, and this and that. And you know what is so strange, is there is no one in professional baseball that is batting a thousand. I doubt there is anyone batting six hundred. There is no one probably batting even five hundred. But as long as you're not afraid in life, and step up and take on a challenge, you never know what is going to happen. And every challenge that I have been faced with, I am going to step up and swing. Because one time I may hit a home run. And that home run is going to carry me a little bit farther.

◆ *Herschel Walker*

We never know how high we are
Till we are asked to rise
And then if we are true to plan
Our statures touch the skies

The Heroism we recite
Would be a normal thing
Did not ourselves the Cubits warp
For fear to be a King—

◆ *Emily Dickinson*

Oh man! There is no planet, sun or star could hold you, if you but knew what you are.

◆ *Ralph Waldo Emerson*

When you are inspired by some great purpose, some extraordinary project, all your thoughts break their bounds: your mind transcends limitations, your consciousness expands in every direction and you find yourself in a new, great and wonderful world. Dormant forces, faculties and talents become alive, and you discover yourself to be a greater person by far than you ever dreamed yourself to be.

◆ *Patanjali*

No guts, no glory.

◆ *Author unknown*

As you go along your own road in life, you will, if you aim high enough, also meet resistance, for as Robert Kennedy once said, "If there's nobody in your way, it's because you're not going anywhere." But no matter how tough the opposition may seem, have courage still—and persevere.

There is no doubt, if you aim high enough, that you will be confronted by those who say that your efforts to change the world or improve the lot of those around you do not mean much in the grand scheme of things. But no matter how impotent you may sometimes feel, have courage still—and persevere.

It is certain, if you aim high enough, that you will find your strongest beliefs ridiculed and challenged; principles that you cherish may be derisively dismissed by those claiming to be more practical or realistic than you. But no matter how weary you may become in persuading others to see the value in what you value, have courage still—and persevere.

Inevitably, if you aim high enough, you will be buffeted by demands of family, friends and employment that will conspire to distract you from your course. But no matter how difficult it may be to meet the commitments you have made, have courage still—and persevere.

It has been said that all work that is worth anything is done in faith.

◆ *Madeleine K. Albright*

If you travel through Europe today, you will see—in every city and in many villages—cathedrals of stirring beauty and incomparable durability. Created eight centuries or more ago, these remarkable structures remain as inspiring, as graceful, and even as functional as when they first were built.

But they are more than architectural masterpieces. They tell us something about the human spirit. These cathedrals were built at a time when life was turbulent and uncertain. War, violence, and disease were continual threats. All the organized institutions of society were oppressive to all but a privileged few. Illiteracy was virtually universal. There was little time and few resources for anything but survival. Yet, the desire to create something beautiful and lasting would not be suppressed.

When a town built a cathedral, everyone participated. The young and strong dug the foundations; masons laid the stones; others crafted the metal, sculpted the statues, polished the bells. The work went on for decades, even centuries. Therefore, many of the people involved knew they would never see the finished building. Yet, they wanted to be part of it.

The cathedrals of Europe are only an example of this urge to create, to build something for future generations, and to express beauty. It manifests itself in every nation, every culture, every faith. It is the flint that strikes fire in our souls and brings forth art, literature, and poetry. And it is the reason we pursue education.

So the question I think each of you must contemplate this morning is: "What kind of cathedrals will I build?"

On a day like this one, we can all feel a powerful sense of excitement. The air is almost electric, isn't it? You may think that feeling is relief, because you have passed the last exam or—if you're a parent—paid the last bill.

But I think it is something more. It is the excitement of meeting the greatest challenge of your life. Like a superbly trained athlete who is eager for the competition to start, you are ready now for the real thing. You don't know what the outcome will be, but you have prepared yourself, and you are ready to test your skills and your character.

But your profession is only one dimension of your true self. Whether or not you pursue a career, the rest of a well-spent life must be devoted to learning—about your fellow human beings, about the world around you, about yourself. Have you yet tested all your abilities and limitations? Have you experienced all the things you hope to feel? Have you satisfied all your curiosities? I sincerely hope not, because I feel like I have barely begun.

Each of you has a unique combination of attributes—skills, talent, intelligence, personality, ambition—with which you will build your cathedrals. One of the determinants of your success will be how well you understand the full spectrum of your own personal qualities.

What you can share in common are certain virtues that are valid in any age. Among these are honesty, compassion, fairness, self-discipline, and a sense of responsibility to you and to others. I would add one more virtue to that list: Optimism.

Believe in the perfectibility of your fellow human beings. Believe that your own hard work will be rewarded. Believe that you can make a difference. Believe that you can create a better world for the children who will follow you. Above all, believe in yourself.

Steven C. Beering

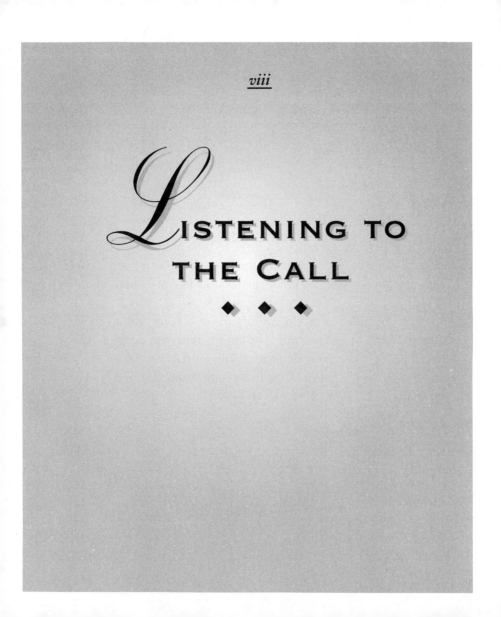

Listening to the Call

◆   ◆   ◆

♦ ♦ ♦

A lot of parents want their children to be something—a doctor or a lawyer. I wanted to be a comedian. But what does that mean to people? My mother would always say, "Oh, he makes a fool of himself and gets paid for it."

. . . I remember as a kid sitting in a restaurant, eating a pizza, watching a party of about six people. One of them was going on about something, and the rest of them were laughing so hard the food was falling out of their mouths. It was like a light went on inside my head. I said to myself: *"That's what it's about."*

. . . You know, it's all because I wanted to be accepted. That's why I tell jokes. I discovered that people would laugh at my jokes, and that meant they *liked* me, they accepted me. It was even better when they started throwing *money.*

♦ *Bill Cosby*

There is some place where your specialties can shine. Somewhere that difference can be expressed. It's up to you to find it, and you can.

♦ *David Viscott*

The return from your work must be the satisfaction which that work brings you and the world's need of that work. With this, life is heaven, or as near heaven as you can get. Without this—with work which you despise, which bores you, and which the world does not need—this life is hell.

◆ *W. E. B. Du Bois*

The person who does not work for the love of work but only for money is not likely to make money nor to find much fun in life.

◆ *Charles M. Schwab*

Once I asked my counselor for advice about my vocation. I asked, "How can I know if God is calling me and for what he is calling me?" He answered, "You will know by your happiness. If you are happy with the idea that God calls you to serve him and your neighbor, this will be the proof of your vocation."

◆ *Mother Teresa*

I wanted so badly to study ballet, but it was really all about wearing the tutu.

◆ *Elle MacPherson*

It is very dangerous to go into eternity with possibilities which one has oneself prevented from becoming realities. A possibility is a hint from God. One must follow it.

◆ *Søren Kierkegaard*

Life is raw material. We are artisans. We can sculpt our existence into something beautiful, or debase it into ugliness. It's in our hands.

◆ *Cathy Better*

Up to a point a man's life is shaped by environment, heredity, and movements and changes in the world about him; then there comes a time when it lies within his grasp to shape the clay of his life into the sort of thing he wishes to be. . . . Everyone has it within his power to say, this I am today, that I shall be tomorrow.

◆ *Louis L'Amour*

Just don't give up trying to do what you really want to do. Where there is love and inspiration, I don't think you can go wrong.

◆ *Ella Fitzgerald*

The way I enjoyed spending time most was dancing. That's from the time I was a very small child, when I puttered around the house. When I was four or five years old, I remember already having a regime. It was the way I always identified myself.

◆ *Twyla Tharp*

I loved to write when I was a child. I wrote, but I always thought it was something that you did as a child, then you put away childish things. I thought it was something I would do for fun. I didn't know writers could be real live people, because I never knew any writers.

◆ *Rita Dove*

There is always the danger that we may just do the work for the sake of the work. This is where the respect and the love and the devotion come in—that we do it to God, to Christ, and that's why we try to do it as beautifully as possible.

Mother Teresa

If he only works for himself, he can probably become a famous scholar, a great wise man, an excellent poet, but never a complete, truly great man. History calls great those men who ennoble themselves by working for the general good; experience praises as most fortunate the one who makes the greatest number of people happy; religion itself teaches us that the ideal toward which we all strive has sacrificed itself for humanity, and who would dare to destroy such sayings. If we have chosen the position in which we can do the most for humanity, then burdens can not depress us, because they are only sacrifices for all; then we will not enjoy any poor, limited, selfish joys, but our happiness will belong to millions, our deeds will live quietly but will work on for ever, and our ashes will be dampened by the glowing tears of noble men.

Karl Marx

Do what you love. Do what makes your heart sing. And never do it for the money. Don't go to work to make money; go to work to spread joy. Seek ye first the kingdom of Heaven, and the Maserati will get here when it's supposed to.

Marianne Williamson

THE STAGE

There is only one place in the world where I love to be. The strangest part is that this place is where I am the least myself and not at all alone. It's onstage. Not just standing there looking out over empty seats, but in the middle of a show when I am the most nervous. When I have so many butterflies in my stomach that I feel like I'm about to pee. That pause just before a very dramatic line where the whole audience waits to hear what *I'm* about to say. Or when the stage is completely dark and I can't see a thing except the blinding spotlight in my eye. When I have worked so hard on a part that I have bruises to show for it. That's where I'm truly happy.

I love late-night practices, where I have worked for such a long time that I begin to forget my lines out of fatigue. When a part dares me to try something new. Or at tryouts, when I'm watching all the other girls trying out for the part I want, and notice that I know how to do it better. Opening night when I don't know how the audience is going to respond. This is where I find my high.

The smell of makeup in the air. Rushing around making sure everything is ready for me when I go on. The heat of the stage lights on your skin. Dusty old costumes that someone said would look fine from offstage. Becoming someone completely different than who I really am. Letting myself be taken over by the character I play, and forgetting myself in it all.

This is my calling, my passion, my place.

◆ *Megan Biolchini*

Don't let anyone think little of you because you are young.... Be sure to use the abilities God has given—put those abilities to work.

I Timothy 4:12, 14

Everything on the earth has a purpose, every disease an herb to cure it, and every person a mission.

Mourning Dove

[The first time I was onstage] I was a teapot. I was a small teapot, short and stout, here was my handle, this was my spout. And I was like seven. It was the greatest. I was just bowing, and bowing. They had to come get me off the stage. I just kept bowing. "Thank you, thank you, thank you, thank you." You know. All the other pots are gone. Born ham, that's basically me.

Whoopi Goldberg

Make your life a mission—not an intermission.

Arnold H. Glasgow

I think knowing what you cannot do is more important than knowing what you can.

Lucille Ball

Hide not your talents. They for use were made. What's a sundial in the shade?

Benjamin Franklin

Man's biggest mistake is to believe that he's working for someone else.

◆ *Nashua Cavalier*

Real joy comes not from ease or riches or from the praise of men, but from doing something worthwhile.

◆ *Pierre Corneille*

It's a job—someone's gotta do it. The reality is, Jennifer and I can do our job well because we truly are friends. But when the day's over, she goes home to her boyfriend and I go home to a magazine. [On what it's like kissing *Friends* costar Jennifer Aniston]

◆ *David Schwimmer*

Work for the fun of it, and the money will arrive some day.

◆ *Ronnie Milsap*

Desire! That's the one secret of every man's career. Not education. Not being born with hidden talents. Desire.

◆ *Bobby Unser*

I just wake up and say, "You're a bum, go do something worthwhile today."

◆ *Garth Brooks*

Make your work to be in keeping with your purpose.

◆ *Leonardo da Vinci*

At the age of six I wanted to be a cook. At seven I wanted to be Napoleon. And my ambition has been growing steadily ever since.

◆ *Salvador Dalí*

When I was a little kid I thought I would grow up to be black and sing jazz in nightclubs.

◆ *Molly Ringwald*

The decision as to what your career is to be is a very deep and important one, and it has to do with something like a spiritual requirement and commitment.

◆ *Joseph Campbell*

God doesn't give people talents that he doesn't want people to use.

◆ *Iron Eagle*

You were born to greatness. Having a life mission implies that the world has need of you. In fact, the world has been preparing you to fill this need with one incredible life experience after another. Finding and fulfilling your potential will lead to your highest experience in this life. Believe it, you have a mission. It is the gateway to your personal greatness. . . . It may also seem difficult to believe that you were born to greatness. You were. You have the ability to develop majesty of character. You have the capacity for self-love. And you can serve with love, the highest sign of greatness.

◆ *Greg Anderson*

Initially I wanted to be Muhammad Ali. But then I got into a fight and I got my butt kicked, so I figured I could choose something else.

◆ *Kenneth "Babyface" Edmonds*

The secret of success is making your vocation your vacation.

◆ *Mark Twain*

That is what is lost in so many lives, and what must be recovered: a sense of personal calling, that there is a reason I am alive.

◆ *James Hillman*

Is that what they call a vocation, what you do with joy as if you had fire in your heart, the devil in your body?

◆ *Josephine Baker*

We are here to do what there is a deep psychological and emotional imperative for us to do. That's our point of power, the source of our brilliance. Our power is not rationally or willfully called forth. It's a divine dispensation, an act of grace.

◆ *Marianne Williamson*

We must trust our soul's noncallings as well as its callings. Destiny seems to have very specific ideas about what each of us should be doing on the planet, and our greatest personal fulfillment always lies in those directions and none other.

◆ *Dianne Skafte*

Far and away the best prize that life offers is the chance to work hard at work worth doing.

Theodore Roosevelt

Think enthusiastically about everything; but especially about your job. If you do so, you'll put a touch of glory in your life. If you love your job with enthusiasm, you'll shake it to pieces.

Norman Vincent Peale

Blessed is he who has found his work. Let him ask no other blessing.

Thomas Carlyle

I don't know what your destiny will be, but one thing I know: the only ones among you who will be really happy are those who have sought and found how to serve.

Albert Schweitzer

To have a great purpose to work for, a purpose larger than ourselves, is one of the secrets of making life significant, for then the meaning and worth of the individual overflow his personal borders and survive his death.

Will Durant

It is the first of all problems for a man to find out what kind of work he is to do in this universe.

Thomas Carlyle

If you do what you like, you never really work. Your work is your play.

Hans Selye

Few will have the greatness to bend history itself, but each of us can work to change a small portion of events.

Robert E. Kennedy

If you can't do it with love and cheerfulness, don't do it at all—go home.

Mother Teresa

There's no labor a man can do that's undignified, if he does it right.

Bill Cosby

Without work, all life goes rotten. But when work is soulless, life stifles and dies.

Albert Camus

The trouble with the rat race is that even if you win you're still a rat.

Lily Tomlin

Every man has his own vocation; talent is the call.

Ralph Waldo Emerson

Work to become, not to acquire.

Elbert Hubbard

Every calling is great when greatly pursued.

Oliver Wendell Holmes

Consciously or unconsciously, every one of us does render some service or other. If we cultivate the habit of doing this service deliberately, our desire for service will steadily grow stronger, and will make, not only for our own happiness, but that of the world at large.

Mahatma Gandhi

The world makes way for the person who knows where he or she is going.

Ralph Waldo Emerson

In order that people may be happy in their work, these three things are needed: They must be fit for it; they must not do too much of it; and they must have a sense of success in it.

John Ruskin

I always knew, since I was like four. I wanted to be Barbra Streisand. I wanted to be in Broadway shows. I was the only fourth grader who knew all the worlds to *South Pacific*. . . . There was never a second choice for me—it was showbiz or nothing.

Rosie O'Donnell

The majority work to make a living; some work to acquire wealth or fame, while a few work because there is something within them which demands expression. . . . Only a few truly love it.

◆ *Edmond Boreaux Szekely*

I think the person who takes a job in order to live—that is to say, for the money—has turned himself into a slave. Work begins when you don't like what you're doing. There's a wise saying: make your hobby your source of income. Then there's no such thing as work, and there's no such thing as getting tired. That's been my own experience. I did just what I wanted to do. It takes a little courage at first, because who the hell wants you to do just what you want to do; they've all got a lot of plans for you. But you can make it happen. I think it's very important for a young person to have the courage to do what seems to him significant in his life, and not just take a job in order to make money. But this takes a bit of prudence and very careful planning, and may delay financial achievement and comfortable living. But the ultimate result will be very much to his pleasure.

◆ *Joseph Campbell*

I don't believe that man was born to work for a living; I believe he was born to make what he lives for his work.

◆ *Les Brown*

Love your calling with passion, it is the meaning of your life.

◆ *Auguste Rodin*

I remember in college, everybody talking about how they were going to get jobs. I thought, "Geez, I don't want to get a job. That doesn't seem like any fun. I've been having fun. I want to keep having fun." So I said, "Is there some sort of job out there where you can just fool around and have fun?"

◆ *Jerry Seinfeld*

It is the paradox of life that the way to miss pleasure is to seek it first. The very first condition of lasting happiness is that a life should be full of purpose, aiming at something outside self.

◆ *Hugh Black*

Many persons have a wrong idea of what constitutes true happiness. It is not attained through self-gratification but through fidelity to a worthy purpose.

◆ *Helen Keller*

And all work is empty save when there is love; and when you work with love you bind yourself to yourself, and to one another, and to God.

◆ *Kahlil Gibran*

No man has ever risen to the real stature of spiritual manhood until he has found that it is kinder to serve somebody else than it is to serve himself.

◆ *Woodrow Wilson*

Don't be satisfied with stories, how things have gone with others. Unfold your own myth.

◆ *Rumi*

It's amazing how many cares one loses when one decides not to be something, but to be someone.

◆ *Coco Chanel*

The first duty of a human being is to find your real job and do it.

◆ *Charlotte Perkins Gilman*

For the sake of making a living we forget to live.

◆ *Margaret Fuller*

No one else can tell you what your life's work is, but it's important that you find it. There is a part of you that knows—affirm that part.

◆ *Willis Harman*

The most radical, powerful act ever undertaken by any human being remains the act of committing oneself, beyond reservation, to a worthy personal mission.

◆ *Christopher Childs*

Find the passion. It takes great passion and great energy to do anything creative. I would go so far as to say you can't do it without that passion.

◆ *Agnes de Mille*

No man . . . can be a genius; but all men have a genius, to be served or disobeyed at their own peril.

◆ *Ananda Coomaraswamy*

Everyone has his own specific vocation or mission in life to carry out a concrete assignment which demands fulfillment. Therein he cannot be replaced, nor can his life be repeated. Thus, everyone's task is as unique as is his specific opportunity to implement it.

◆ *Viktor Frankl*

Profound joy of the heart is like a magnet that indicates the path of life. One has to follow it, even though one enters into a way full of difficulties.

◆ *Mother Teresa*

The fun of being alive is realizing you have a talent and you can use it every day so it grows stronger. . . . And if you're in an atmosphere where this talent is appreciated instead of just tolerated, why, it's just as good as sex.

◆ *Lou Centrilivre*

If a man has a talent and cannot use it, he has failed. If he has a talent and uses only half of it, he has partly failed. If he has a talent and learns somehow to use the whole of it, he has gloriously succeeded, and won a satisfaction and a triumph few men ever know.

◆ *Thomas Wolfe*

I've always known where I wanted to go in life. I've never let anything deter me. This is my purpose. It will unfold.

◆ *Tiger Woods*

The road to happiness lies in two simple principles: find what interests you and that you can do well, and put your whole soul into it—every bit of energy and ambition and natural ability you have.

◆ *John D. Rockefeller III*

I think I was chosen by basketball. . . . I think that my God-given physical attributes, big hands, and big feet, the way that I'm built, pro-portion-wise, just made basketball the most inviting sport for me to play. . . . It was a two-way street. I liked the game, I enjoyed the game, and the game fed me enough, and gave me enough rewards to reinforce that this is something that I should spend time doing, and that I could possibly make a priority in my life, versus other sports.

◆ *Julius Erving*

I'd rather be a failure at something I enjoy than a success at something I hate.

◆ *George Burns*

After fifty years of living, it occurs to me that the most significant thing that people do is go to work, whether it is to go to work on their novel or at the assembly plant or fixing somebody's teeth.

◆ *Thomas McGuane*

I long to accomplish a great and noble task, but it is my chief duty to accomplish small tasks as if they were great and noble. The world is moved along, not only by the mighty shoves of its heroes, but also by the aggregate of the tiny pushes of each honest worker.

◆ *Helen Keller*

When young people tell me they don't know what they want to do with their lives, I explain that they should concentrate on finding out about life first. Some people have to try several directions before they find the one that is right for them. There is nothing wrong about this.

◆ *Joyce Brothers*

Our work is meant to be a grace. It is a blessing and a gift, even a surprise and an act of unconditional love, toward the community—and not just the present community that may or may not compensate us for our work, but the community to come, the generations that follow our work.

◆ *Matthew Fox*

Life is to be lived. If you have to support yourself, you had bloody well better find some way that is going to be interesting. And you don't do that by sitting around wondering about yourself.

◆ *Katharine Hepburn*

Don't go around saying the world owes you a living; the world owes you nothing; it was here first.

◆ *Mark Twain*

Since I was twenty-four there never was any vagueness in my plans or ideas as to what God's work was for me.

Florence Nightingale

The white light streams down to be broken up by those human prisms into all the colors of the rainbow. Take your own color in the pattern and be just that.

Charles R. Brown

Starting out to make money is the greatest mistake in life. Do what you feel you have a flair for doing, and if you are good enough at it, the money will come.

Greer Garson

Any path is only a path. There is no affront to yourself or others in dropping it if that is what your heart tells you to do. But your decision to keep on the path or to leave it must be free of fear and ambition. I warn you: Look at every path closely and deliberately. Try it as many times as you think necessary. Then ask yourself and yourself alone one question. It is this: Does the path have a heart?. . . Does this path have a heart is the only question. If it does, then the path is good. If it doesn't, it is of no use.

Carlos Castaneda

If you're going to be a failure, at least be one at something you enjoy.

Sylvester Stallone

It is better to start late on the right job than to spend a frustrating and mediocre life in the wrong one.

M. T. Harrington

Your work is to discover your work and then with all your heart to give yourself to it.

Buddha

The truth is that all of us attain the greatest success and happiness possible in this life whenever we use our native capacities to their greatest extent.

Smiley Blanton

Work is an essential part of being alive. Your work is your identity. It tells who you are. It's gotten so abstract. People don't work for the sake of working. They're working for a car, a new house, or a vacation. It's not the work itself that's important to them. There's such joy doing work well.

Kay Stipkin

The essential conditions of everything you do must be choice, love, passion.

Nadia Boulanger

Work is love made visible.

Kahlil Gibran

Never work just for money. Money will not save your soul or build a decent family or help you sleep at night. We are the richest nation on earth with the highest incarceration and one of the highest drug addiction and child poverty rates in the world.

Marian Wright Edelman

There is no higher religion than human service. To work for the common good is the greatest creed.

Albert Schweitzer

If a person's work is to live, it must come from the depths of him or her—not from alien sources outside oneself—but from within.

Meister Eckhart

Of all the paths a man could strike into, there is, at any given moment, a best path . . . a thing which, here and now, it were of all things wisest for him to do . . . to find this path, and walk in it, is the one thing needful for him.

Thomas Carlyle

Work is a four-letter word. It's up to us to decide whether that four-letter word reads "drag" or "love." Most work is a drag because it doesn't nourish our souls. The key is to trust your heart to move where your talents can flourish. This old world will really spin when work becomes a joyous expression of the soul.

Al Sacharov

Only he who keeps his eye fixed on the far horizon will find his right road.

◆ *Dag Hammarskjöld*

I believe there's an inner power that makes winners or losers. And the winners are the ones who really listen to the truth of their hearts.

◆ *Sylvester Stallone*

Every man has his own destiny; the only imperative is to follow it, to accept it, no matter where it leads him.

◆ *Henry Miller*

Every one is born into the world to do something unique and something distinctive and if he or she does not do it, it will never be done.

◆ *Benjamin E. Mays*

There is in every one of us something that waits and listens for the sound of the genuine in ourselves, and it is the only true guide you'll ever have. And if you cannot hear it, you will all of your life spend your days on the ends of strings that somebody else pulls.

◆ *Howard Thurman*

Every human being has a work to do, duties to perform, influence to exert, which are peculiarly his, and which no conscience but his own can teach.

◆ *William Ellery Channing*

Our world is incomplete until each one of us discovers what moves us—our passion. No other person can hear our calling. We must listen and act on it for ourselves.

◆ *Richard J. Leider*

Do what you can, with what you have, where you are.

◆ *Theodore Roosevelt*

To be successful, the first thing to do is fall in love with your work.

◆ *Sister Mary Lauretta*

Remember, a job is something you do for money, but a career is something you do out of love. Chase your passion, not your pension!

◆ *Dennis Kimbro*

The high prize of life, the crowning fortune of man, is to be born with a bias to some pursuit which finds him in employment and happiness.

◆ *Ralph Waldo Emerson*

They are happy men whose natures sort with their vocations.

◆ *Francis Bacon*

We will discover the nature of our particular genius when we stop trying to conform to our own or to other people's models, learn to be ourselves, and allow our natural channel to open.

◆ *Shakti Gawain*

Blessed is he who has found his work; let him ask no other blessedness. He has a work, a life-purpose. . . . Get your happiness out of your work or you will never know what real happiness is. . . . Even in the meanest sorts of labor, the whole soul of a man is composed into a kind of real harmony the instant he sets himself to work.

Thomas Carlyle

The best career advice to give the young is, "Find out what you like doing best and get someone to pay you for doing it."

Katharine Whitehorn

We are not here to make a living. We are here to enrich the world, and we impoverish ourselves if we forget this errand.

Woodrow Wilson

The noblest question in the world is, What Good may I do in it?

Benjamin Franklin

It is your work in life that is the ultimate seduction.

Pablo Picasso

The most unhappy of all men is the man who cannot tell what he is going to do, who has no work cut out for him in the world and does not go into it. For work is the grand cure of all the maladies and miseries that ever beset mankind.

Thomas Carlyle

Work for your soul's sake.

◆ *Edgar Lee Masters*

It isn't really important to decide when you are very young just exactly what you want to become when you grow up. It is much more important to decide on the way you want to live. If you are going to be honest with yourself and honest with your friends, if you are going to get involved with causes which are good for others, not only for yourself, then it seems to me that that is sufficient, and maybe what you will be is only a matter of chance.

◆ *Golda Meir*

I think the purpose of life is to be useful, to be responsible, to be honorable, to be compassionate. It is, after all, to matter: to count, to stand for something, to have made some difference that you lived at all.

◆ *Leo C. Rosten*

Always you have been told that work is a curse and labor a misfortune. But I say to you that when you work you fulfill a part of earth's furthest
dream, assigned to you when that dream was born,
And in keeping yourself with labour you are in truth loving life,
And to love life through labor is to be intimate with life's inmost secret.

◆ *Kahlil Gibran*

Great minds have purposes, others have wishes.

◆ *Washington Irving*

If you follow your bliss,
you will always have your bliss,
money or not.

If you follow money,
you may lose it,
and you will have nothing.

◆ *Joseph Campbell*

We are challenged on every hand to work untiringly to achieve excellence in our lifework. Not all men are called to specialized or professional jobs; even fewer rise to the heights of genius in the arts and sciences; many are called to be laborers in factories, fields, and streets. But no work is insignificant. All work that uplifts humanity has dignity and importance and should be undertaken with painstaking excellence. If a man is called to be a streetsweeper, he should sweep streets even as Michelangelo painted, or Beethoven composed music, or Shakespeare wrote poetry. He should sweep streets so well that all the hosts of heaven and earth will pause to say, "Here lived a great streetsweeper who did his job well."

◆ *Martin Luther King, Jr.*

I am a firm believer in the theory that people only do their best at things they truly enjoy. It is difficult to excel at something you don't enjoy.

◆ *Jack Nicklaus*

The Bible has taught us, metaphysics has taught us, myth has taught us, that if you get into the flow, if you do what you're supposed to do, you'll be rewarded with riches you've never imagined. What I have received is the natural order of things. You would be shocked as to what you can accomplish when you rid yourself of the slave mentality.

◆ *Oprah Winfrey*

Every individual has a place to fill in the world and is important in some respect, whether he chooses to be so or not.

◆ *Nathaniel Hawthorne*

I think a poet is a workman. I think Shakespeare was a workman. And God's a workman. I don't think there's anything better than a workman.

◆ *Laurence Olivier*

To find out what one is fitted to do, and to secure an opportunity to do it, is the key to happiness.

◆ *John Dewey*

It seems to be that the person with a spiritual perspective has a unique advantage for fulfilling his or her mission. Love gives such people constant direction, a true-north compass point toward which they can travel without fail. If we simply ask, "What's the loving thing to do?" the next step in implementing our mission becomes increasingly clear.

◆ *Greg Anderson*

This is your life, not someone else's. It is your own feeling of what is important, not what people will say. Sooner or later, you are bound to discover that you cannot please all of the people around you all of the time. Some of them will attribute to you motives you never dreamed of. Some of them will misinterpret your words and actions, making them completely alien to you. So you had better learn fairly early that you must not expect to have everyone understand what you say and what you do. The important thing is to be sure that those who love you, whether family or friends, understand as nearly as you can make them understand. If they believe in you, they will trust your motives. But do not ask or expect to have anyone with you on everything. Do not try for it. To reach such a state of unanimity would mean that you would risk losing your own individuality to attain it.

◆ *Eleanor Roosevelt*

People who make a living doing something they don't enjoy wouldn't even be happy with a one-day work week.

◆ *Duke Ellington*

Happiness lies not in the mere possession of money; it lies in the joy of achievement, in the thrill of creative effort. The joy and moral stimulation of work no longer must be forgotten in the mad chase of evanescent profits. These dark days will be worth all they cost us if they teach us that our true destiny is not to be ministered unto but to minister to ourselves and to our fellow men.

◆ *Franklin D. Roosevelt*

There can be no richer man or woman than the individual who has found his or her labor of love. Personal fulfillment through the virtue of work is the highest form of desire. Work is the conduit between the supply and the demand of all human needs, the forerunner of human progress, and the medium by which the imagination is given the wings of action. A labor of love is exalted because it provides joy and self-expression to those who perform it.

◆ *Dennis Kimbro*

Everybody can be great. Because anybody can serve. You don't have to have a college degree to serve. You don't have to make your subject and verb agree to serve. You don't have to know about Plato and Aristotle to serve. You don't have to know Einstein's theory of relativity to serve. You don't have to know the second theory of thermodynamics in physics to serve. You only need a heart full of grace. A soul generated by love.

◆ *Martin Luther King, Jr.*

When I look back on it now, if I'd have gone to art school, or stayed in anthropology, I probably would have ended up back in film. No matter which route I would have taken, I'm almost positive I would have ended up eventually in film.

Mostly I just followed my inner feelings and passions, and said, "I like this, and I like this," and I just kept going to where it got warmer and warmer, until it finally got hot, and then that's where I was.

◆ *George Lucas*

Forever at his door
I gave my heart and soul. My fortune too.
I've no flock any more,
no other work in view.
My occupation: love. It's all I do.

St. John of the Cross

You can be relatively certain that if you hate doing something, it is not your vocation. Joseph Campbell constantly advised people who had lost their way to follow their bliss. Augustine said, "Love and do what you want." The exercise of those gifts that define the path with heart will produce delight. Of course, there are as many different strokes as there are different folks. I know people for whom tuning an engine is a vocation, cooking a fine soup, designing an elegant house, running a day-care center, nursing the terminally sick, running a political campaign, raising organic garlic. I know of few jobs or professions that are not spiritual callings for some who practice them.

Sam Keen

None of us needs instruction in how to recognize what our heart is saying. We do need guidance, however, on how to have the courage to follow those feelings, since they will force us to change our lives in any case. But consider the consequences of not listening to the heart's guidance: depression, confusion, and the wretched feeling that we are not on our life's true path, but viewing it from a distance.

Caroline Myss

We want our lives to catch fire and burn blue, not smolder. We want to use ourselves up, leave this life the way we entered it—complete—and die with a yes on our lips and not a no, making that last transition, that final threshold, with some grace, with eyes wide open and not squeezed shut as if for a blow. We don't want to enter kingdom come kicking and screaming and begging for more time. Following our calls is one way to love our lives, to flood them with light that can shine back out of them, and to make life easier to explain to ourselves when it's over and we're wondering "What was that all about?" By following our calls, we just may be able to face death more squarely. Although we may never really be ready for it, we'll never be readier.

◆ *Gregg Levoy*

There is a vitality, a life force, a quickening that is translated through you into action, and because there is only one of you in all time, this expression is unique. And if you block it, it will never exist through any other medium and be lost. The world will not have it. It is not your business to determine how good it is, nor how valuable it is, nor how it compares with other expressions. It is your business to keep it yours clearly and directly, to keep the channel open. You do not even have to believe in yourself or your work. You have to keep yourself open and aware directly to the urges that motivate you. Keep the channel open.

◆ *Martha Graham*

I'm convinced that my job situation is a model of the future. This chapter is being written as I sit alone in my home office in my pajamas....

When you work alone, everything is optional, including clothes. I can do dangerous things if I want to. I can do dangerous things naked if I want to. I can sexually harass myself while doing dangerous things naked. And I can insult myself for doing it. Best yet, I can do it during the time I've scheduled for my own staff meeting. I try to do all of those things as often as possible.

Scott Adams

To attempt to make a career choice, apart from an examination of our values and apart from a consideration of the impact that our doing has upon society, is to make an immature choice. It is immature because it lacks the confidence to face up to one's responsibility to mankind. "They" are never going to make the world a better place. It's up to you and me, and we *can* do it—if we have the love, the courage, and the patience.

We must have the love to go for what we know is right, even if it means paying a price. We who love life must work with life for life, while celebrating the mystery that is life. In short, we must be actively engaged in making the world the best it can be, while loving it exactly as it is. We must have the courage to believe that the world we have dreamed will one day be made manifest and that what we do as individuals makes a difference. We must have the courage to reject the idea of settling for work that is destructive to human happiness, or even indifferent to it.

Laurence G. Boldt

WORK THOU FOR PLEASURE

Work thou for pleasure; paint or sing or carve
The thing thou lovest, though the body starve.
Who works for glory misses oft the goal;
Who works for work's sake then, and it well may be
That these things shall be added unto thee.

◆ *Kenyon Cox*

"You know what I'd like to be?" I said. "You know what I'd like to be? I mean if I had my goddam choice? . . . You know that song 'If a body catch a body comin' through the rye'? . . . I keep picturing all these little kids playing some game in this big field of rye and all. Thousands of little kids, and nobody's around—nobody big, I mean—except me. And I'm standing on the edge of some crazy cliff. What I have to do, I have to catch everybody if they start to go over the cliff— I mean if they're running and they don't look where they're going I have to come out from somewhere and catch them. That's all I'd do all day. I'd just be the catcher in the rye and all. I know it's crazy, but that's the only thing I'd really like to be."

◆ *J. D. Salinger*

What every man needs, regardless of his job or the kind of work he is doing, is a vision of what his place is and may be. He needs an objective and a purpose. He needs a feeling and a belief that he has some worthwhile thing to do. What this is no one can tell him. It must be his own creation. Its success will be measured by the nature of his vision, what he has done to equip himself, and how well he has performed along the line of its development.

Joseph M. Dodge

Futurists suggest that the average high school graduate will have six careers in her lifetime. That's not jobs! That's careers! If you are interested in trying something new, take the time to do it. What's the worst that can happen? You might invest a small amount of time in an activity that ends up having little payoff. But most of us waste more time than that daily watching commercials on TV. The potential cost of experimenting with what life has to offer is small compared to what can be gained.

Terry L. Paulson &
Sean D. Paulson

Everybody has talent, it's just a matter of moving around until you've discovered what it is. A talent is a combination of something you love a great deal, something you can lose yourself in—something that you can start at nine in the morning, look up from your work and it's ten o'clock at night—and something that you have a natural ability to do very well. And usually those two things go together.

You know, a lot of people like to do certain things, but they're not that good at it. Keep going through the things that you like to do, until you find something that you actually seem to be extremely good at. It can be anything. There's lots and lots and lots of different things out there. It's a matter of moving around until you find the one for you, the niche that you fit into.

◆ *George Lucas*

That's what you really have to look for in life, something that you like, and something that you think you're pretty good at. And if you can put those two things together, then you're on the right track, and just drive on.

Once you've got something that you like, something you're good at, then do it for all it's worth. Be the very best you can be. Let nothing deter you; let nothing stand in your way, and go for it.

◆ *Gen. Colin L. Powell*

The way to find out about your happiness is to keep your mind on those moments when you feel most happy, when you really are happy—not excited, not just thrilled, but deeply happy. This requires a little bit of self-analysis. What is it that makes you happy? Stay with it, no matter what people tell you. This is what I call "following your bliss." . . . I always tell my students, go where your body and soul want to go. When you have the feeling, then stay with it, and don't let anyone throw you off. . . . We are having experiences all the time which may on occasion render some sense of this, a little intuition of where your bliss is. Grab it. No one can tell you what it is going to be. You have to learn to recognize your own depth. . . . I even have a superstition that has grown on me . . . if you do follow your bliss you put yourself on a kind of track that has been there all the while, waiting for you, and the life that you ought to be living is the one you are living. When you see that, you begin to meet people who are in the field of your bliss, and they open the doors to you. I say, follow your bliss and don't be afraid, and doors will open where you didn't know they were going to be.

Joseph Campbell

When I was five years old I would lie in bed, look at the radio, and I wanted to be on the radio. I don't know why. I was magically attuned to it. I would listen to these voices, and then as I got a little older—and just a little older, seven or eight—I would imagine myself doing what they were doing. I would actually stand up, sit down, I'd go to the mirror, and I would say, "The Romance of Helen Trent," as if I were the announcer. Then I would go to baseball games and I'd roll up the score card, and I'd sit up in the back row, and all my friends would look up at me, and I'd broadcast the game to myself. I fantasized being a broadcaster.

Larry King

What I know is, is that . . . if you do work that you love, and work that fulfills you, the rest will come. You know you are on the road to success if you would do your job, and not be paid for it. And I would do this job, and take on a second job to make ends meet if nobody paid me. Just for the opportunity to do it. That's how you know you are doing the right thing.

Oprah Winfrey

If I can stop one Heart from breaking
I shall not live in vain
If I can ease one Life the aching
Or cool one Pain

Or help one fainting Robin
Unto his Nest again
I shall not live in vain.

Emily Dickinson

HOW TO BE HAPPY . . .

Last year as I was finishing up my semester in Argentina, I put together a little "yearbook" for the others who had studied with me. I did this in my last week there, while writing final papers, saying good-bye to new, but dear, friends and places, and packing everything I had brought and all that I had acquired back into my two suitcases.

The yearbook wasn't fancy; I didn't have time to even put in pictures. I just collected people's addresses, favorite quotes, their superlatives as voted by the others, and what they wanted to be when they grew up. I remember distinctly what one woman wrote as her desired occupation: happy. She wanted to be happy when she grew up.

Once again we're packing up a lot of memories along with our belongings and preparing to go far away—mentally if not physically. Many of us, here and now, are also thinking that question: "What do I want to be when I grow up?" I guess you could say that we're along the way to being grown up, although I plan at least a few more decades of growing before I'm officially there. But now is probably a good time to think about what we want to be when we grow up. And happy doesn't sound like too bad of a goal, does it?

So let's talk about happiness, or rather how we can go toward that goal. I think we can all agree that to be happy we should live a positive life. That makes sense. So, how then can we make sure that we live positively? One way is to surround ourselves with positive things and positive experiences. Read good books, see good movies, have beautiful artwork hanging on our walls. We should eat delicious food, buy ourselves fresh flowers to greet us when we get home, and attend all kinds of concerts frequently.

It is important to remember why we are living on this earth. What are our priorities: our family and friends or getting that extra bonus by working one hundred hours a week? Which really and truly makes us happier? We only have one life, so let's treat ourselves well, with massages and bubble baths. Never pass a playground without stopping to swing. Throw away our watches and maybe even try living without a planner for a day. Find the little things, like sunrises and sunsets, or tequila shots and pet rocks, that make a day worth living. And always, always, always have a reason to get out of bed in the morning—whether it's the brownies you baked the night before or the realization that Thursday means *ER* is on at 10:00.

That way of positive living doesn't sound too bad, does it? But I'd like to introduce another way of living positively. This previous way is inward-looking. The goal is to bring positive or happy things of the world into our lives. A second manner of positive living is more outward-focused. The goal is to direct our own positivity (if I can take the liberty of inventing a word) onto the world. To perhaps even seek out the negative things in this world and work to make them positive.

This lifestyle might not appear so much fun, at first. We no longer can claim that it is for "positive" reasons that we don't read the bad news in the newspaper. To the contrary, we must open our eyes and ears to what is happening in all corners of this world that is our global community. Sure, it does no good to numb ourselves to all the horrors of the world by repeated contact. But we cannot solve problems without knowing they are there.

In this life, maybe instead of going to a concert, you will perform for others. Maybe instead of buying cut flowers, you will plant flowers in a vacant lot for others to enjoy. Maybe you will teach, heal, counsel, raise a child, or write policy that changes the world. Building a house with Habitat for Humanity may come before that weekend at the spa. But look at what you've made at the end of a day! The beautiful artwork that a schoolteacher hangs on her wall may come from a yet undiscovered talent. But when it is given to you in appreciation of your love, there is no art so beautiful in the world! The hours at the rape crisis center are not always conducive to watching sunsets. When you take responsibility for the world, bubble baths sometimes have to wait.

I cannot tell you what to do in your life. You must find your own causes, based on your own convictions. Each of us must use our own talent and our own strengths to give what we can. But each of us must give.

Think again about why we are here on earth and what is really important in life. What is the most positive way you can lead your life? As I said before, the key to a positive life is to always, always, and always have a reason to get up in the morning. I know of no better reason than that you are needed and that the world will be a better place for your having lived.

Congratulations. I wish you all the happiness in the world.

Janet Hostetler

In saying yes to our calls, we bring flesh to word and form to faith. We bring substance to dreams, to passions, and to the ancient urgencies. We ground ourselves in life and bring ourselves into being as alchemists and magicians in their finest hours. By following our calls, we come as close as seems possible to embodying the gods and knowing some of what it means to have their power—to make bodies out of clay, rain out of vapors, gold out of lead, fruit out of the idea of fruit. We touch dolls with a wand and make their wooden eyes flutter. We give life. By doing so, we please the gods and the goddesses. It is as if we're their very arms and legs, and when we act with enthusiasm, we set them to dancing.

Gregg Levoy

I AM. . . .

I am an architect: I've built a solid foundation; and each year I go to that school I add another floor of wisdom and knowledge.

I am a sculptor: I've shaped my morals and philosophies according to the clay of right and wrong.

I am a painter: With each new idea I express, I paint a new hue in the world's multitude of colors.

I am a scientist: Each day that passes by, I gather new data, make important observations, and experiment with new concepts and ideas.

I am an astrologist: reading and analyzing the palms of life and each new person I encounter.

I am an astronaut: constantly exploring and broadening my horizons.

I am a doctor: I heal those who turn to me for consultation and advice, and I bring out the vitality in those who seem lifeless.

I am a lawyer: I'm not afraid to stand up for the inevitable and basic rights of myself and all others.

I am a police officer: I always watch out for others' welfare and I am always on the scene preventing fights and keeping the peace.

I am a teacher: By my example others learn the importance of determination, dedication, and hard work.

I am a mathematician: making sure I conquer each one of my problems with correct solutions.

PEANUTS © United Feature Syndicate. Reprinted by Permission.

I am a detective: peering through my two lenses, searching for meaning and significance in the mysteries of life.

I am a jury member: judging others and their situations only after I've heard and understood the entire story.

I am a banker: Others share their trust and values with me and never lose interest.

I am a hockey player: watching out for and dodging those who try to block my goal.

I am a marathon runner: full of energy, always moving and ready for the next challenge.

I am a mountain climber: Slowly but surely I am making my way to the top.

I am a tightrope walker: Carefully and stealthily I pace myself through every rough time, but I always make it safely to the end.

I am a millionaire: rich in love, sincerity, and compassion, and I own a wealth of knowledge, wisdom, experience, and insight that is priceless.

Most important, I am me.

Amy Yerkes

Finding and creating your life's work, even if it is entirely different from what you have done most of your life, will bring you more happiness and wealth than any other action you can take. If your primary responsibility in life is being true to yourself, that can only be accomplished by carrying out what you are called to do—your unique and special vocation. The true American dream not only provides the freedom to use your gifts and talents to achieve your highest goal but also gives you the freedom to fulfill your purpose in life. You are meant to work in ways that suit you, drawing on your natural talents and gifts. This work, when you find it and commit to it—even if only as a hobby— is the key to happiness. Your life's work involves *doing what you love* and *loving what you do.*

◆ *Dennis Kimbro*

Permissions and Acknowledgments

Grateful acknowledgment is made to the authors and publishers for the use of the following material. Every effort has been made to contact original sources. If notified, the publisher will be pleased to rectify an omission in future editions.

Madelaine Albright for "As you go along."

Jane Alexander for "My Sons and Daughters in Spirit."

Andrea Brown Literary Agency Inc. for "Louise Coyle" from *Class Dismissed II*, copyright © 1986 by Mel Glenn, reprinted by permission of the author.

Robert D. Ballard for "Perhaps one of the reasons."

Steven C. Beering for "If you travel."

Rosin Bergdoll for "Forever Best Friends."

Megan Biolchini for "Start Here" and "The Stage."

Blue Mountain Arts for "This is one of those rare moments" by Pamela Koehlinger; "I have loved" by Peggy Selig; "Always believe in yourself, Son" by Dena Dilaconi; and "You Can Go as Far as Your Dreams Can Take You" by Colin McCarty, copyright © Blue Mountain Arts Inc., reprinted with permission of Blue Mountain Arts Inc.

Emily Browning for "No Hurry."

Barbara Bush for "Today you meet to say good-bye."

George Bush for "Don't be afraid of trying."

Colleen Clyder for "Separate Ways" and "Looking Back."

Dove Books for "The Dance" from *Dreams into Action.* Copyright © 1996 by Milton Katselas. Reprinted with permission of Dove Books.

Isabelle Evans for "It's over."

Robanne Frederickson for "My mom always said."

Bill Frist for "Be eager to dream."

Johndavid Galindo for "I Can't Live Without Her."

Ellen Goodman for "There's a trick."

Rina Harbison for "Childhood Dreams."

Health Communications Inc. for "The Gift" by Renee R. Vroman from *A 3rd Serving of Chicken Soup for the Soul,* copyright © 1996, reprinted with permission of Health Communications Inc.; for "Growing" by Brooke Mueller; "New Beginnings" by Paula (Bachleda) Koskey; and "I Am . . ." by Amy Yerkes from *Chicken Soup for the Teenage Soul,* copyright © 1997, reprinted with permission of Health Communications Inc.

Janet Hostetler for "Last year as I was finishing."

James S. Hunt for "Some people see."

Paul Irwin for "Dear Kaycie."

Gary Kawasaki for "Speaking to you today."

Kelly Leddy for "A teenage girl."

Christopher Lee for "How Can I Explain?"

Steve Lodle for "People at occasions like this."

Mindy May for "When the details."

Alexandria Miller for "One Picture in a Yearbook."

Michele Ownbey for "A Memory Away."

Raj Patel for "The Ways of Life."

Neil Simon for "There is one last bit of advice."

Dennis R. Tesdell for "Life is All Too Short: Ways to Make It the Best It Can Be," Web site at http://www.coachdt.com.

Henry Matthew Ward for "Commencement."

Scott C. Wilcox for "Paraphrasing the words."

Winston-Derek Publishers for "Goal" by Don B. Decker in *Successful Strategies for Your Life,* copyright © 1995, reprinted with permission of Winston-Derek Publishers.